OPTION TRADING

In Your Spare Time

A Guide to Financial Independence for Women

Wendy Kirkland and Virginia McCullough

SPHINX® PUBLISHING
AN IMPRINT OF SOURCEBOOKS, INC.®
NAPERVILLE, ILLINOIS
www.SphinxLegal.com

Published by: **Sphinx® Publishing, An Imprint of Sourcebooks, Inc.®**
P.O. Box 4410
Naperville, Illinois 60567–4410
(630) 961–3900
Fax: (630) 961–2168
www.sourcebooks.com

Library of Congress Cataloging-in-Publication Data

Kirkland, Wendy.
  Option trading in your spare time / Wendy Kirkland and Virginia McCullough.
    p. cm.
  Includes indexes.
  1. Commodity futures–United States. 2. Options (Finance)–United States. I. McCullough,
Virginia. II. Title.
  HG6049.K54 2009
  332.63'2283–dc22
                                2009011861

Printed and bound in the United States of America.
VP 10 9 8 7 6 5 4 3 2

DEDICATION

Wendy wishes to dedicate this book to Jack, who released and propelled her like a kite so she could experience flight, but whose gentle hand kept her from flying too far away.

Virginia dedicates this book to her children, Laura and Adam, who are always the light of her life.

CONTENTS

Why Purchase Stock Options?

A Critical Tool for a Successful Trading Plan

What Do You See?

What Made the First Cut?

Back to Your List and IBD

Checking for Ripeness with *Technical Screens*

Trend Trading–Examining Trends

Simple Moving Averages (SMAs)

Understanding Option Chains

Long and Short Moving Average Crossovers

Relative Strength Index (RSI)

Understanding Volume

Understanding Gaps

Understanding Oscillators

Williams %R

Moving Average Convergence and Divergence (MACD)

Percentage Price Oscillator (PPO)

Understanding Stochastics

Average Directional Index (ADX)

Accumulation/Distribution Line

Applying the Principle behind Puts

The Big and Small Pictures Count

What to Keep Your Eye On

A Strategy in Action

Buy Signals–Calls

Buy Signals–Puts

Keep Your Eye on the Charts

Another Chart to Analyze

Let's Look for More Opportunities

Looking at a Well-Known Company

A NASDAQ Stock

Looking at Another Sector

Looking at ETFs and the Option Index

What is your frame of mind—your mental approach—when you
   make an investment?
How are taxes on profits and losses handled?
Can you form a business around option trading?
Is option trading completely an isolated, individual endeavor?
What qualities do you think good traders share?
Are you involved in the market all the time?
Do some women trade only ETFs?
Do you have a favorite stock or a list of stocks you particularly like?
How do you handle losses on an emotional level?
How much of your investment fund do you have invested at any
   one time? And how much on any one stock?
Do you watch the stock channels on TV? And if so, how do you
   filter the information?
If an option contract drops to the point that it has no value at its
   expiration date, do you have to close it, so that you don't have
   to exercise the option to buy the stock?
Are there option traders who day trade?
When you sell an option contract, are those funds available
   immediately to reinvest?
What would you say is the most valuable lesson you have learned?
What would you say has been your biggest mistake?
Can a person make a living trading options?

ACKNOWLEDGMENTS

The "path to empowerment" has been made smoother by the efforts and support of many people. My love and sincere appreciation goes to them all. My buddy Rachelle Rogers first shined her light on option trading and introduced me to Robin Laylon, my first options instructor. Robin helped me build a firm foundation and provided tools for success. My good friend Virginia McCullough agreed to walk at my side as we placed our feet on the path.

Most importantly, Jack, my husband, lover, and friend, has supported my efforts and encouraged me for forty-three years. My three children, Kim, Leslie, and Patrick, have always stood on the sidelines cheering me on, saying, "Go girl. You can do it." Likewise, my brother and sister-in-law, Jeff and Peg Roulston, let me know that even if I should stumble, the landing will be cushioned by their love and support. And finally, I thank my dad, Abbott Lieberman, my first exploration mentor. He taught me that anything worth doing holds risk, and how I experience the journey is my choice, so go make it a happy day!

–Wendy Kirkland
Asheville, North Carolina
2009

PREFACE

My friend leaned across the table at the restaurant where we'd met for lunch. Then she glanced around the room, as if making sure no one could hear her. "I'm involved in something new—and very exciting," she whispered.

"Oh? Is it a secret?" From the way she was acting, I thought she must be talking about a new relationship or perhaps a "change your life" seminar that offered the keys to lasting happiness or something equally momentous.

She shook her head. "No, not at all, but sometimes people don't believe me." She stopped talking long enough to take a deep breath. "Okay, here goes. In seven days, I made a 55% profit trading options on eBay stock."

"You did what?" I had to follow the nouns, so to speak—55% profit, options, eBay stock. I had no idea how one could—legally—make a 55% profit on anything in a week. But that day my friend explained it to me in brief terms, and by the time I went back to the store I own with my husband, Jack, I'd eagerly agreed to take a class and explore the world of option trading. I felt as if I'd been given a chance to jump on board a train with a very appealing destination.

I was also a bit confused, even bewildered. Jack and I have owned and operated a retail gift store for more than twenty years, so I have a good understanding of profit margins. I know how difficult it is to find those hard-earned numbers after deducting escalating expenses. For sure, our profit comes in single or *low* double-digit figures, and our business is considered quite successful.

Over these past twenty years in our particular business, which is dependent on a steady flow of tourists in our locale, Jack and I have kept the doors open seven days a week, and in that time, we've raised three kids, paid our mortgage, and contributed to their college fees and other expenses. We've loved being our own bosses, and that's the key to what kept us going during some very difficult times. (That same deep desire for independence also piqued my interest in trading options.)

We consider ourselves fortunate in most ways, but the downside of our life hit home more and more as we crept up on our retirement years. I realized that we'd been so busy working, plodding along the path of our well-grooved life, and being the kind of supportive parents and grandparents we thought we should be, we'd left ourselves out of the equation. We invested in our business, but we'd failed to invest in ourselves and our future.

Like many millions of Americans, we had *opened* a retirement account to which we were supposed to make regular deposits or at least contribute a lump sum at the end of each year. Somehow, though, things always got in the way. One year it was a wedding and the next year one of our grandchildren needed help only a specific private school could provide. The next year, we had a major car repair and we ordered extra inventory for the business at a great price. It was always something! Every new challenge that came up loomed with greater immediacy than that meager and languishing retirement fund. Besides, until a few years ago, retirement seemed light-years away.

I don't want to leave the impression that I never thought ahead. I often daydreamed about my so-called golden years. In my fantasy life, I imagined I'd be a rather happy retiree, free to spend quality time talking to my tomato and pepper plants and dressing my perfect dog in galoshes and a raincoat when we went out for walks in the rain. I also planned to spend even more hours in front of the computer writing interesting stories.

These flights of imagination might have continued, but to tell you the truth, I'd started to lose sleep from worry. I tried asking for a sign and affirming that I'd soon have the answer; I even visualized an arrow pointing in the right direction. I figured that without some kind of dramatic flash of intuition that would lead to an entirely new opportunity, I'd be working until I dropped—and that would probably happen between waiting on a customer and borrowing from one account to pay a bill on another.

You see, I'd started counting on something new coming into my life, because the well-known and logical choices were not practical in our case. We already worked very long hours—more hours than we knew were healthy. We had a great store location, but within a few percentage points, our receipts have remained more or less the same year after year–our square footage was giving all that it could give. Our revenues went slightly down if a nearby street was closed for construction and slightly up if the weather cooperated with a special event in town. We'd cut back our expenses as far as we could and that still wasn't enough to provide the extra income we needed for our future.

We were stuck in a rut that we'd been carving for years, yet it was a groove Jack and I were comfortable walking–we knew the terrain. I also felt sure that at this stage in my life, I didn't want to begin a new career, and even if I could have managed it, I didn't want to explore a new franchise or open a second location or move to a larger one. I certainly didn't want to take on a home-based sales business that involved leaning on my friends to host parties so I could sell pretty lingerie or the best garlic press or storage container in the world to reluctant guests. I'd already firmly rejected the pyramid schemes that acquaintances tried to sell me on from time to time. Besides, taking on another twenty hour-a-week part-time job was out of the question. If I did that, when would I see my family and friends?

I became acutely aware that no one cared more about my future than I did, that no one cared more about my money than I did, and I needed a path where I was in control.

Frustration and anxiety mounted–not to mention my blood pressure–until that day my friend talked about the "exciting" venture that had captured her attention and, in a short time, brought her rich rewards. Needless to say, I was primed and ready to hear more. She explained that a class on option trading was being offered locally at a cost of $400, which some quick research told me was very inexpensive compared to the cost of Internet courses on option trading–and the weekend seminar prices can really soar. (Even more important, the high cost of these other classes and seminars left the impression that you had to have a lot of money to make money. My experiences with option trading speak volumes in countering that notion.)

My friend also explained that after a five-week course and some time spent practicing, she'd quickly recouped her expenses and was well on her way to *supplementing her income*. Ah, the magic words I needed to hear! The arrow had appeared and was pointing the way to the class.

I performed a sleight of hand, or put another way, I robbed Peter to pay Paul and managed to secure the fee for the course. I took the first class, and walked away knowing in my gut, my heart, and my head that trading options would be a good fit for me. I had nothing to lose but the time it would take to learn more.

Over the following weeks, I realized that I had at long last found a way to make additional money without working more hours and without the need to invest in special equipment, search for a new location, hire employees, or buy inventory. I didn't need to build in costs like advertising or utilities, and I wasn't asking anyone else to buy or sell something. I could actually do the research and trade options at my gift shop, in my kitchen, while visiting our kids, or virtually any other location that had a computer and Internet connection.

After completing the course, I opened a trading account with $800, which, as you probably know, is a relatively small amount of money with which to begin investing. Yet, the amount is also quite typical among the individuals I've encountered since I've been involved with option trading. Without question, taking the course, devoting some time practicing the skill, and completing a few profitable trades worked together to firmly set my feet on a new path.

My trading funds have multiplied exponentially, and with my profits I've regularly funded our retirement account. So you see, trading options doesn't replace other forms of investing. More importantly, though, the path I'm walking has widened and become much more interesting because of the women I've encountered who are curious about this area of investing and crave more information. I found I had a knack for teaching to match my knack for trading, and after coaching others one-on-one and getting groups of women together to learn and share the adventure, this book resulted.

My long-time friend, Virginia McCullough, happened to be one of the women I talked with about my experiences, and she, too, believed that a book offered a way to approach this topic in a manner that removed the mystique from option trading. Again and again, I came back to the concept of women's empowerment, and a book seemed like a logical step.

Still, why did I believe that women in particular would respond to this information? After all, nothing in the basic information applies only to women or has some special meaning to women. Certainly, men trade options every day. However, once I became involved in option trading, I began to notice ads for weekend seminars on option trading–and there was nothing inherently wrong with them. But the fees for option trading seminars were high–many running several thousand dollars. The more I understood about option trading, the more I realized that these seminars often hyped options as a mystery and claimed to have the key to unlock their secrets.

One direct mail piece I received opened the sales letter with "Dear Fellow Betting Man." This about sums up the problem with most of the advertisements I saw about trading options. They act as if this is a macho adventure, filled with exciting risk–like white water rafting! They at least imply that trading options is reserved for an elite group who have the guts to take it on. Worse, some who sell seminars and newsletters play off the idea that the stock market has allure for the "hard-driving, gamblin' man." Please. If we want the supposed thrill of betting, we'll go to the racetrack or buy a ticket to Vegas. Or we can stay home and buy a lottery ticket for $1 and take our chances.

In contrast, I asked myself how many women would like to stay home with their young kids and operate a part-time business. How many women are looking ahead to retirement, but can't hope to have the money to travel or build fabulous new homes like the people they see on TV commercials for brokerage firms? How many families are without health insurance because it's priced so high that it's out of reach? I imagine some women simply want to earn enough extra money to pay for a solo or family vacation–and they'd rather not place a few bets at the racetrack in the hopes of scraping together the money.

More and more, I've realized that the beauty of option trading is that like virtually all businesses, it has the ability to expand and contract. It is possible for a woman to trade options because she wants to buy a new couch or a whole new house. For me, this has come down to the fact that trading options has expanded the financial possibilities for me and my family. This is what motivates me to pass on what I know and support women who are looking for greater financial empowerment. And what better way to do this than through a book, along with a supporting website?

No one cares more about your future than you do.

No one cares more about your money than you do.

You've taken the first step on the path to financial empowerment, putting you in control.

However, like other types of investing, patience is required. We have to be patient with ourselves as we learn the particular ways to gather information and analyze what options to buy and sell. Just like the clichés about not building Rome in a day and the long journey starting with a single step, option trading is learned by studying the principles and learning some basic facts about the stock market and individual stocks. It requires a commitment to learning the language of trading and for some, overcoming the fear of the stock market and investing in general. It also requires that we understand the modern world of online transactions and become familiar with online trading services and accounts. This book presents all this information step-by-step, with all the concepts building on each other. (You'll soon notice that we repeat that guideline many times.)

On the upside, because of *virtual trading*, this is an area of investing that can be *practiced* online without spending a penny, and when the investor is ready, a small amount of money–even less than $1,000–offers a good start.

One caveat: before you turn the page and immerse yourself in the information, we want you to be clear about what option trading *is* and equally important what it is *not*:

- **First, it's very important that you start investing with money you can spare.** Do not invest the mortgage payment or school tuition.

- **Second, this is not a get rich quick scheme.** It *is* a sound investment system to add income and gain a good return on investment steadily over time.

- **Third, sometimes people call investing a gamble, but this is not gambling, nor is option trading like standing in line for a lottery ticket.** It *is a reasoned, researched, and educated way of investing varying amounts of money.* You won't invest any money until you've educated yourself and done the research.

So, that said, roll up your sleeves and let's get started. Welcome to the fascinating world of option trading!

–Wendy Kirkland
Asheville, North Carolina
May 2009

Chapter One

THE BASICS

Let's jump right in. First, every trader's education begins with language–the terminology of option trading. If you understand the terms, the door swings open to an understanding of the ways option trading tools work. In addition, most business and financial sectors have government rules and regulations, and as a place to begin, you need a basic understanding of the way option trading is regulated and overseen.

Too often, the financial markets seem confusing, often to the point that many people believe only experts can understand and work with them. However, we found these issues easier to comprehend and absorb if we remove the cloak of mystery that keeps financial markets at a distance.

Wendy likes to say that option trading is a blend of:

- *mathematics*–the calculations and specifics about the markets and individual stocks;

- *art*–the visual dimension that allows you to *see* the big picture;

- *history*–how the market and individual companies perform over varying intervals of time; and,

- *psychology*–the field that helps you understand market trends and your own investing style.

Fortunately, you don't have to be an expert in these fields. Rather, you'll use a technical analysis along with a system–a plan–to make sound trading decisions.

The visual dimension allows you to absorb a great deal of information, which you'll quickly understand and analyze. The data, including the mathematical information and the charts, may be gathered on the computer, but the success comes from what you bring to it–your ability to use what you learn to make good decisions.

Your Mindset

Imagine walking into an art museum gallery and spotting a painting by one of the masters. The visual center of your brain first processes the painting by taking in the image as a whole, before other parts of the brain get involved in evaluating and analyzing it. Your brain is trained to compile and blend the images, and your gaze lingers in one place only if one area has an element that you find particularly interesting and draws your attention.

This *observing mindset* is where we start when we begin to trade. Then, through experience we program our brains to sift through information and let go of what isn't important in order to leave behind the meaty nuggets. This is the information we use to make creative, informed trading decisions, as we move from the curious mindset to discover the *art* of trading.

Starting the Journey

We know from experience that the best and easiest way to begin the journey into option trading is to approach it as we would a world of its own that gives up its secrets one at a time. Many people, even those who trade stocks regularly, consider the stock market itself a big mystery, an enigma, which is why we think it's the best place to begin. What's actually behind the symbols and numbers we see on the crawls at the bottom of the TV screen or in the columns of fine print we see in the newspaper?

To reduce the stock market to its simplest terms, it is a place where buyers and sellers come together to make exchanges. A transaction at a store–where goods are offered at prices people are willing to pay–and the stock exchange as a whole, have much in common. The difference is that exchanges or transactions on the stock market are less tangible, and in addition, the perceived value of a stock often has little to do with actual worth. Still, the concept of an exchange remains the same.

Fluctuations in the Market

What brings on fluctuations in the markets? In essence, while buyers and sellers come to an agreement on price, they do not always agree on value. In terms of stocks, a trade takes place when one buyer is eager to sell stock at the same time another buyer wants to purchase. Often, after a stock drops in price, a stockholder is anxious to get rid of the security, while another trader sees the drop in price as an opportunity to purchase an undervalued stock. A well-known adage proves true here: one investor's junk is another investor's treasure.

Price versus value is subjective. One company's stock price may trade at sixteen times its earnings and will be considered undervalued with room to grow. Another company's stock may trade at six times its earning and will be considered overpriced and at its peak. There are other influences that illustrate this difference in evaluation. An analyst group (Goldman Sachs, for example) may upgrade a stock based on their expectation of future earnings for that company and the stock's price will soar. Nothing has actually changed to bring about this increase in value, except an expectation, a belief that good things are apt to happen. If this hope is not realized, the stock will drop back to its actual worth or even below that level for a time, until the next event.

These Things Called Stocks

Modern economies offer any number of investment choices–vehicles through which we put money to use to make profits, earn interest, preserve value, create portfolio growth, and so forth. From interest-bearing checking and money-market accounts to treasury bills (T-bills) to municipal bonds, we have many investment choices.

The stock market is the place where individual investors (people and companies) own a share of the action and own a share of the risk, too. Their ownership is measured in increments or units called *stocks*. When companies sell shares of stock, they are selling a share of ownership in that business or conglomerate of businesses.

If you buy one hundred shares of stock of one of the major U.S. corporations, such as Microsoft or Starbucks or Ford Motor Company, you are a shareholder. For as long as you hold the stock, the value of your *portfolio,* defined as your group of investments, regardless of type, gains value or loses value as the price of that stock goes up and down. If you paid $50 per share, and a year later your stock traded at $55 per share, your portfolio value has increased by $500. If the stock is trading at $40 a share, then your portfolio is $1,000 lighter.

Some stocks pay their investors *dividends,* which is the way they distribute the profits. If your one hundred shares of stock–which for discussion's sake we'll say is priced at $50–pay a $1 dividend per share, then every quarter, you will receive $100, which you can reinvest or take as income.

Of course, these are basic definitions and provide the structure and function of stocks. The way stocks work in the everyday world of the stock exchange is a more complex issue. For example, if we were limited to studying and choosing among, let's say, fifty companies, then we could all keep track of what companies are profitable and which are going out of business, and who is merging with whom, and so forth. But, in the U.S. alone, thousands of companies sell shares of their stock, and the profitability of these companies is influenced by factors that no single individual or event can control. That's why financial services companies, including brokerage firms, hire analysts whose job involves watching trends and using complex formulas to determine short-term and long-term profitability.

Mutual funds are groups of stocks (or bonds or a mix of stocks and bonds) that came into being as a way to allow average people a chance to own stock in a variety of companies, thus reducing the risk involved with owning shares of individual stocks. Many 401(k) employee retirement accounts and IRAs (Individual Retirement Accounts) have money invested primarily in mutual funds. These are popular instruments because they allow investors to turn over the day-to-day overseeing of the mutual funds to managers who analyze and follow the trends, and if successful, increase their value.

Mutual funds also are further specialized. Some invest in technology or health sectors, others buy blocks of stock in only small or large companies, some take greater risks to achieve greater profits and some take a more conservative approach.

Shopping with the Bulls and Bears

If a major industry comes to your town and brings new jobs and adds money to the economy, then chances are the stores in your area will see an increase in business. If your town loses a major employer, the local stores may report a decrease in business because less money is circulating.

Likewise, economic trends that influence the markets and stocks have a herd effect, so to speak. When economic trends are on the rise and stocks are increasing in value because investors are confident, then we're said to be in a *bull market.* On the other hand, in times of great economic change or uncertainty, or when a dramatic event makes the market jittery, then stocks may decline in value, and analysts say we're in a *bear market.*

Of course, stocks rise and fall on a daily basis, and we don't assign the terms *bull* or *bear* based on a day or a week's performance. And the terms are relative, as well. The market can be bearish for a period of time when other economic forecasts seem uncertain. On the other hand, the market can turn bullish when certain indicators point to economic expansion. (These indicators and trends are a study in themselves, but for now, the general definitions will do.)

Sometimes, individual investing professionals are known to be good at predicting bull or bear markets; some investors are known as *bulls* because they tend to do well when markets are good–they have a good nose for sensing when to buy. Others are known as *bears* because they anticipate declines in the market and hence, when to sell and preserve their profits.

Adding Options to the Mix

First, *options* are vehicles we use to move in and out and through the stock market. An *option* is the right–but not the obligation–to buy or sell a security at a certain price before a certain expiration date. (For our purpose, stocks are the *security*.)

There are options in many different arenas where option trading is carried out, including stocks, indexes, future contracts, commodities, securities, and so forth. However, you don't need to concern yourself with all the possible areas in which you can trade options. This book is devoted to a discussion in these three areas–stocks, exchange traded funds (ETFs), and indexes. (We'll define the terms later.)

There are two types of options–call options (call) and put options (put).

- *Call options* are contracts that give the owner the right, but not the obligation, to buy a specified number of shares of a security at a specified price, called the *strike price*, on or before a specified date, called the *expiration date*. Call options are purchased when the price of the underlying stock is expected to go up.

- *Put options* are contracts that give the owner the right, but not the obligation, to sell a specified number of shares of a stock at a specified price, the *strike price*, on or before a specified date, the *expiration date*. Put options are purchased when the price of the underlying stock is expected to go down.

The Trend Is Your Friend

The concepts of bulls and bears become relevant here. In a *bull market,* when the overall market is going up, successful option traders buy and sell call options. It is counterproductive to go against the flow of the market, or, to express this concept another way, it doesn't make sense to ignore the upward bias of the market. Likewise, in a *bear market,* when the overall market is trending to lower stock prices, then successful option traders consider purchasing put options.

For now, we'll confine our discussion to call options and will save an in-depth look at put options for Chapter 6.

Note: You are buying and selling options to buy and sell stock, but you don't exercise the option. In other words, you will not own shares of the stocks on which you purchase options.

The *strike price* is what the underlying stock will be sold or bought for if the option is exercised. (Keep reading, because the chart that appears soon will start to clarify this.) As we said, we're purchasing options on what is called the *underlying instrument,* referred to as the *underlying.* In the context of this book, the underlying is a stock, an ETF, or an index.

The underlying is identified by its *symbol.* If you see the financial news crawls on the TV stations, such as CNBC, you'll see the symbols crawling past. The newspapers also identify stocks by their symbols. For example, MasterCard's symbol is MA, IBM's symbol is IBM, and so on.

The number of letters in the symbol matters and tells us something about the stock.

- *One, two, or three letters* means it is a Dow Jones stock, listed on either the New York Stock Exchange (NYSE) or the American Stock Exchange (AMEX).

- *Four or five letters* in its symbols means it is a NASDAQ stock.

If we put all the definitions together, we complete the definition of an option.

So, let's look at MA Sept 130 Call. This is a call option to buy MasterCard (the underlying stock) at a price of $130 (the strike price) at any time through the September expiration date (the expiration date is always the third Friday of the expiration month).

Example

Let's say you have a friend who wants to sell her house for $100,000. You are familiar with the neighborhood and you like the park-like green space that makes the area desirable, but you don't have the $100,000 to purchase the house as an investment, so you offer another proposal. "If you'll give me a piece of paper saying I can purchase your house for $100,000 anytime over the next twelve months," you say to your friend, "I will give you an extra $10,000." Your friend agrees to your proposal, because it's not important that she sell today. In essence, you have bought an option.

Six months later, a shopping center is under construction a half-mile away, making the properties in the area in hot demand. Now the house has gone up in price to $120,000. You hold up your paper–the option–and wave it in front of interested buyers. "I'll sell you this paper for $15,000. It states that you can purchase this $120,000 house for only $100,000."

Someone takes you up on your offer, and the trade is made. Here's what happened.

- Your friend receives the $100,000 she wanted for her house, in addition to the $10,000 you paid for the option to purchase her property.

- The new buyer purchases a house valued at $120,000 for $100,000 plus the $15,000 he paid you for the paper option. He pays a total of $115,000, a savings to him of $5,000.

- And, you receive $15,000 for the option (paper) you purchased for $10,000 six months ago, so you made a $5,000 profit on your $10,000 investment.

- That means that you realized an astounding 50% return within six months.

This story illustrates in a concrete way the crux of the secret world of trading options. In our story, you see the house, the owner, and the buyer. They are all tangible to you. In the world of stocks, it's all like pieces of paper, so to speak. However, the principle is the same. *You control enough of a great stock to make a great deal of money with essentially only a down payment.*

Most of us can't go out and simply plunk down $100,000 to invest in an *underlying instrument,* like a second house or a block of stocks. But we can benefit from the leverage of controlling the *underlying* with a fraction of the house or stock cost by using options.

What Can You Expect from Trading Options?

You can achieve significant short-term profits on the funds you invest in the options market. You make your profits by purchasing option contracts–calls and puts–with the express intention of selling the contract after the underlying, the stock, ETF, or index, has moved in price, either up, as with calls, or down, as with puts, and you sell well before the option's expiration date. When you purchase a green banana from the produce market, you know the banana still has a while before it has to be eaten. In terms of options, the idea is to sell the banana before it becomes yellow with brown spots, soft and ready to expire.

As you see, by using this strategy, you never exercise your option to buy the underlying stock. Your goal is to hold the option long enough for the price of the underlying stock to increase in the case of a call option or decrease in price in the case of a put option. You don't intend to exercise the option, but someone else will want to, *and that's its value.*

Note: Our *option premium* is the amount we pay to control the underlying stock. This option premium increases in a magnified way when compared with the underlying stock price. As the stock price goes up so, too, our option increases in value, and then we sell our option to someone else, well before the expiration date. In that way, we trade the options, but never actually buy or sell the underlying stock.

Remember these two crucial points:

1.   As option traders, we make money by purchasing the right to buy or sell a thing, and that right in itself has value and gives us, the traders, leveraging power.

2.   We never need to worry about finding an interested buyer; through the option contract itself, the sale is guaranteed the moment that you decide to sell.

Because most of us are accustomed to thinking of the stock market as the store in which we buy and own actual shares of stock, and then decide to sell for various reasons, it sometimes requires a new mindset to fully appreciate the word *option*. That deal you pulled off on the house–your $5,000 profit in six months–probably sounds pretty good. Let's see what it would look like with a stock option.

When you buy an option on a stock, you can think of the option as a down payment on that stock. We'll purchase an option on one hundred shares of MasterCard stock to control the financial power of those one hundred shares.

To make this even clearer, let's compare a stock purchase to an option purchase:

- If MasterCard's (MA) stock price is $100 per share, one hundred shares of stock would cost $10,000. If next month, the stock price goes up $2 and we sell the stock, we have a profit of $200 on our one hundred shares. Our profit is 2%.

- But, if we buy a call option on those same one hundred shares of MA stock, we will pay approximately $600. (This is a good estimate, but the actual option prices vary greatly). This $600 controls all one hundred shares of the stock. If MasterCard's stock price goes up $2, your option may also go up $2. (This, too, varies according to the underlying option). This $2 increase or $200 profit is 33% of the initial price you paid for the option. Using the leverage of options, *you've made 33% profit on the same underlying instrument (stock) that only realized (gained) a 2% profit when the actual stock was sold.*

  100 shares @ $100 = $10,000
  $2 increase x 100 shares = $200
  New Value = $10,200
  Gain = 2%
  Or
  1 Option contract on 100 shares @ $6 per share = $600
  $2 increase in option price x 100 shares = $200
  New Value = $800
  Gain = 33%

As you can see so far, options provide traders with certain benefits. For example, you can begin trading with a small amount of money and can turn a high percentage of profit.

As your confidence increases, you can earn even greater profits. With careful, precise trading, a $200 profit can become $400, $400 can become $800, and before long a trading account will increase, showing exponential or *compounded* profit.

The Obvious Question

At this point, everyone wants to know how to decide what stock options to buy. The most obvious answer is that we only purchase options that are expected to achieve a substantial return on our investment. And how do we know that? Once we understand the principles of option trading, then it's time to learn how to carefully consider the underlying stock upon which the option is based. We'll get to that a little later, and we provide a complete discussion in Chapter 3 about a method to select great underlying stocks. Clearly, that's the heart of the matter.

We Have Choices

When we decide to purchase a call option on a stock, we also have the choice to buy in-the-money, at-the-money, or out-of-the-money options. (We have these same choices on put options, which we'll discuss in chapter 6.)

- *In-the-money* is the amount by which the price of the underlying exceeds the strike price. For example, AAPL (Apple Computer's) stock price is $56.50. We decide on a strike price of $50, with a June expiration date. The option contract would read: *AAPL June 50 Call.* This June option is $6.50 *in-the-money*, which is the difference between the stock price and the strike price. The 50 is the strike price of $50 and the expiration date is the third Friday in June. (Again, the expiration is always the third Friday of the expiration month)

- *At-the-money* is the amount when the price of the underlying matches the strike price, or nearly so. For example, AAPL (Apple Computer's) stock price is $50.50. You decide on a strike price of $50, with a June expiration date. The option contract would read: *AAPL June 50 Call.* This June option is *at-the-money,* since the strike price nearly matches the stock price.

- *Out-of-the-money* is the amount by which the price of the underlying is below the strike price. For example, AAPL (Apple Computer's) stock price is $56.50. You decide on a strike price of $60, with a June expiration date. The option contract would read: *AAPL June 60 Call*. This option is $3.50 *out-of-the-money*, since the stock price is below the strike price.

Though the terminology may seem to indicate that the strike price moves, this is not the case. We may say the strike price has moved from out-of-the-money to in-the-money, but it is actually the underlying stock price that has moved. The strike price remains constant, consistent with the price of the option purchased. The *AAPL June 60 Call* remains a $60 call option no matter if AAPL's stock price moves above or below $60.

WMT Wal-Mart Stores, Inc   **48.21** ⊠ **+0.36**

Open: 47.82	High:	48.50
Low: 47.80	Volume:	23,281,285
Yield: 1.83%	P/E Ratio:	15.60
Bid: n/a	Ask:	n/a
Ex Div. Date: 12/12/2007	Ex Div. Amount:	0.22

Pay $9.95. Get the works. | *charles* SCHWAB

OPTION CHAIN FOR WAL-MART STORES, INC

CALLS								PUTS					
					Hide December, 2007 Options								
Symbol	Last	Change	Vol	Bid	Ask	Open Int.	StrikePrice	Symbol	Last	Change	Vol	Bid	Ask	Open Int.
WMTLG	13.20			13.20	13.30	32.00	35.00	WMTXG	0.05				0.05	6,510.00
WMTLU	10.70			10.70	10.80	54.00	37.50	WMTXU	0.05				0.05	4,712.00
WMTLH	8.40	+0.10	8.00	8.20	8.30	69.00	40.00	WMTXH	0.02				0.05	24,526.00
WMTLV	5.70	+0.40	131.00	5.70	5.80	393.00	42.50	WMTXV	0.03				0.05	16,819.00
WMTLI	3.19	+0.39	94.00	3.20	3.30	721.00	45.00	WMTXI	0.01				0.05	34,085.00
WMTLW	0.80	+0.40	3,948.00	0.70	0.80	45,354.00	47.50	WMTXW	0.05	-0.05	2,443.00		0.05	27,337.00
						Stock Price ▶	48.21	Last as of 12/21/2007 4:02:00 PM					
WMTLJ	0.05	+0.02	187.00		0.05	45,370.00	50.00	WMTXJ	1.75	-0.46	270.00	1.70	1.80	13,604.00
WMTLX	0.05				0.05	17,049.00	52.50	WMTXX	4.50	+0.20	10.00	4.20	4.40	161.00
WMTLK	0.05				0.05	7,838.00	55.00	WMTXK	6.85			6.70	6.90	15.00
WMTLY	0.05				0.05	7,730.00	57.50	WMTXY	10.10			9.20	9.40	22.00
WMTLL	0.05				0.05	4,524.00	60.00	WMTXL	11.80	-0.10	69.00	11.70	11.90	1.00
WMTLM	0.08				0.05	51.00	65.00	WMTXM	16.80	-0.10	69.00	16.60	16.90	71.00
WMTLN					0.05		70.00	WMTXN	21.80	-0.10	69.00	21.60	21.90	

All options available to purchase, whether they are *in-, at-*, or *out-of-the-money*, are listed on an option chain. An example of a chain appears above, but do not over-analyze it. We just want to begin to grasp the terminology and to recognize the appearance of these tables and charts. We will cover the specifics of this table as we go along.

This and the information to follow may seem like a lot to take in all at once, and it may even seem like a foreign language. Well, in a sense it is, but in a short time you will be able to appraise the information given in all these charts, tables, and graphs as quickly and easily as scanning a recipe.

Remember, we always provide examples to illustrate, so read through the definitions and don't be concerned if you don't yet grasp the full meaning.

An option's complete *premium* or *price* is comprised of two things, which are then shadowed by another aspect–*intrinsic value* and *time value,* shadowed by volatility. *Intrinsic value* is the in-the-money value. Out-of-the-money options' intrinsic value is zero. The *time value* of an option's price decreases as time passes. Out-of-the-money options are comprised entirely of time value, while a deeply in-the-money option is comprised almost entirely of intrinsic value.

Example

An easy way to understand these terms is to think of a bottle of milk purchased from the supermarket.

- The milk itself has intrinsic value, and the longer the time left before it reaches its sell date, the more time value it has. The combination of the two factors make up its value.

- As the milk closes in on its sell date, its time value decreases, until at expiration it has zero time value and maintains only the intrinsic value of the milk itself.

Note: An option's *premium* (the amount needed to purchase it) is always comprised of its intrinsic value and its time value. If a $100 (strike price) call on IBM costs $10 with IBM's stock price at $108, the intrinsic value of the stock is then $8; therefore, its time value must be $2. Stock price $108–$100 (strike price) = $8 (intrinsic) + $2 (time value) = $10 (premium)

Time value represents the cost of time from the present day of purchase to the date of the associated option's expiration. For example, the cost of a Target (TGT) June 60 call will be more than the cost of a Target April 60 call. In the case of the June 60 call, the cost is more because of the added benefit of having two additional months until expiration.

Why would two extra months be worth paying for? Consider the probabilities involved in price changes in the underlying stock. Is it more likely that the underlying stock will move $2 in one month or in three months?

Because option premium change is largely driven by the change in the underlying stock price (affecting an option's intrinsic value), having more time for the change to happen will be to our advantage and we would expect to pay a higher premium for the benefit of added time.

Enter Volatility

The *shadowing effect* mentioned above is the historical and implied volatility of a stock. Volatility in the stock market refers to the movement in the price of a stock as a function of time as compared with other issues. Historical volatility refers to the actual price movement over time, in the past. An estimation of future price movement is also taken into account in the overall volatility component of option premium pricing and is referred to as implied volatility.

This is not something that you need to mathematically figure out; it is incorporated within option chain pricing, but a general understanding is advantageous. For example, if a stock moves $1 in one day, it is more volatile than a stock that typically moves $1 in a week.

To receive the benefit of this higher relative volatility, we must pay a higher premium for the associated option. This is why an option contract on one particular $100 stock might cost $4, while an option contract on another $100 stock might cost $6 to purchase. The price is higher because the probability of premium appreciation within the lifespan of the option for the faster-moving underlying stock is higher. Our chance of making more money faster grows with higher volatility.

The Simple Principle

The optimum time to *purchase an option contract* occurs while a stock is holding its breath, in a time of calm when the option premium is lower than it might be at other times, and then *sell* when it has increased in value and moves into a more cost-rising volatile period. EX. AAPL 2/14

More Terms to Remember

Before we consider how to use the information, here are some additional terms to absorb.

- *Option Contracts. Option contracts* are always sold in lots controlling one hundred shares of stock. Two option contracts would control two hundred shares of stock, ten option contracts one thousand shares.

- *Option Contract Symbols.* Each option contract or option is given a specific and individual symbol code identifying it: *Underlying Stock Symbol + Expiration Code + Strike Price*

So, using that formula, what does the call option symbol, IBMAJ, mean? This option symbol tells us it's an option on *IBM,* and *A = January,* and *J = $150* Strike Price.

Explanation

This material, the formula designations, might sound confusing, but hang in–the fact is, there is no reason for you to try to remember or memorize any of this, or even fully understand it right now. We've listed them here only to add an element to the full picture. The months follow the alphabet, so B = February, C = March, D = April, and so forth. Likewise, put expiration month symbols begin with M. M = January, N = February, O = March, and so forth. There is no need to memorize these symbols; they are listed here to give you a basic understanding. One might wonder if when this system was derived nearly thirty years ago, it wasn't thought of as a secret code to be decoded only by an elite few.

Month	Call	Put
January	A	M
February	B	N
March	C	O
April	D	P
May	E	Q
June	F	R
July	G	S
August	H	T
September	I	U
October	J	V
November	K	W
December	L	X

Likewise, the strike price value follows the alphabet A = $5. This seems clear enough, in that B would equal ten, until we quickly realize we'll run out of letters before we reach a strike price of say, $150. The table below shows the multiples, but does not illustrate the important fact that price code "A," for example, could mean any of the following strike prices: $5, $105, $205, etc. This is not so much a problem with stocks, because they usually split to stay in the $0 to $100 range (most of the time).

Price Code	Price	Price Code	Price	Price Code	Price
A	05	J	50	S	95
B	10	K	55	T	00
C	15	L	60	U	7.5
D	20	M	65	V	12.5
E	25	N	70	W	17.5
F	30	O	75	X	22.5
G	35	P	80		
H	40	Q	85		
I	45	R	90		

In the same way that "A" can represent different strikes so, too, U–X can represent larger strike prices by adding $30 to their number. U can stand for a strike price of $7.50, $37.50, $67.50, $97.50 etc.

The Chicago Board of Exchange (CBOE) has come up with some root symbols to resolve the multiple-of-$100 ambiguity in its strike price codes, but there is no need to delve into this further, thereby cluttering our minds with the specifics. The only time you might want this information is when you're attending a party or some kind of gathering and you've mentioned that you're an option trader. Some know-it-all is bound to sarcastically ask, "So, do you know what an option symbol means?"

"Easy," you say. "The first letters reflect the underlying (stock), the next letter is the expiration month, and the last is the strike price." Then, you can dust off your hands and move on to mingle with someone more supportive.

As for us, we'll move on to some additional discussion of the stock market. (And please do move on, even if some concepts aren't yet clear to you. We promise, they soon will be.)

Chapter Two

THE STOCK MARKET AND RISK—LOOKING AT TRADING PERSONALITIES

The stock market is made up of a number of parts, each reflecting different sectors of the economy, which, as we can see, define a society and all its activities. The U.S. stock market includes collections of industries (usually referred to as "sectors") that meet the vast needs of almost 300 million people. (The global market reflects the same group of needs/demands.) These sectors include Technology, Gold and Silver, Food, Healthcare, Manufacturing, Biotech, Financial, Energy, Utilities and Transportation.

Each sector is an umbrella covering a variety of industries. For example, the vast Healthcare sector includes businesses involved in medical systems and equipment, nursing homes, pharmaceuticals, HMOs (Healthcare Maintenance Organizations), outpatient and home care, dental supplies, and hospitals, just to name a few. Each of these industries is comprised of companies (of varying sizes) listed on the stock exchanges.

For our purposes as option traders, we'll follow the major trends the big players create. We use the term *big players* to describe the large financial institutions such as mutual funds, brokerage houses, and insurance companies. At times these institutions can feel like a pack of hungry wolves roaming in the forest, and we never want to be in the way of the pack. Our job is to tag along and follow the trail they leave behind that tells us what they're hungry for and which direction they're heading to find it.

What We Watch For

As we follow the big players, we see a couple of things:

- *Trend markets* with large movements in an upward or downward direction over an extended period of time. The trend markets see major reversals several times a year.

- *Trading markets,* which fluctuate in price and direction much faster than trend markets, but less dramatically.

Our trading strategy will be influenced by the type of market we find ourselves in. But always remember that the *volatility,* that is, price variance, is of key importance, because it enables us to realize a profit. Option traders make money as a security escalates in price and as it drops down in price. Ultimately, successful option traders profit because:

- They take the time to learn, understand, and interpret the signs–the clues–the pack leaves behind as they roam the wilds, and

- They make careful decisions, which, contrary to public perception, are *not* based on fear or greed, but rather, are based on our interpretation of the signs and signals initiated by the pack.

Reason and Emotion

One reason that many individuals are afraid of financial markets and investing in general is the language used to describe the mindset involved. For example, if you were to tell a coworker or a neighbor, or even a relative, that you're reading a book on trading options, you might hear comments like, "Oh, I stay away from that roulette wheel," or, "You have to be kidding– why would you risk everything you own on a crapshoot?"

Of course, we realize that you'll also likely encounter others who are seasoned investors and have an understanding of the markets. These individuals may be quite interested in what you're learning and they might want to find out more, too.

However, because of the emotional responses many individuals have to investing and to the financial markets, it's necessary to clarify the mindset that successful investors need. In fact, this is a vitally important topic, and 90% of trading (and other types of investing) success is determined by mental and emotional control. If we don't understand that, we may mistakenly assume that successful traders in either stocks or options are extraordinarily brilliant, lucky, or otherwise in possession of some rare gift. That is not necessarily the truth of the matter.

In fact, sometimes traders talk smart, think smart, but act dumb. By that we mean that they sound technically proficient and they know the lingo and may have a feel for the nuances of the market. Yet, when it comes to the bottom line, the cold reality, many do not consistently make successful trades. Many of these people, brilliant as they may be, are not in control of their emotions.

Wise Option Traders Remember
When left unchecked, emotions will always prod reason to a subservient position.

A trader can be brilliant, but when fear or greed show up, her thinking inevitably becomes distorted. How does this distortion manifest?

Fear of Missing the Party

In this scenario a trader watches the business channels on TV and hears that the market or a stock or a whole sector is making a big move. A TV analyst-anchor confidently offers an explanation of why the move is occurring, and the trader becomes afraid she might miss the party and rushes her decision to purchase an option position.

Another aspect of this fear becomes evident when the novice trader asks for advice and tips from friends, other traders, or Aunt Minnie, but doesn't do her own confirmation. In other words, she doesn't feel confident because she hasn't checked out the information on her own to either confirm it or correct it. She doesn't know what to act on and what to disregard. Still, she's afraid of missing out.

Fear of Taking a Loss

In this scenario, the trader makes the decision to exit an option trade as soon as she sees the slightest blip. After all, if a trade loses any ground, it means that she's made a bad decision and surely the stock and its option will spiral downward. Better to get out now before any loss gets worse.

This fear also can show up when a trader holds a losing position far too long in the hope that it will come back up tomorrow. If she sells at a loss, she admits defeat. This is compounded when a spouse or friend looks on–it's like having an authority figure standing over her shoulder. The trader is afraid and bends to the pressure she feels because that significant person will know she's failed. So, outside accountability can smother good decision-making.

Fear of Losing Profit

Here, a trader holds a winning position too long. She may actually watch an awesome profit erode well after the option position peaked, hoping there will be even greater profit. Because of fear, a 150% profit last week dissipates or becomes a loss the next week.

Fear of Decreasing Profit

In this scenario, this fear might persuade a trader to close a profitable option position too soon.

Note: Keep in mind that among the masses in the investment world, fear moves twice as fast as greed. How do we know that? Well, an option position will drop much faster than it rises. As fear pushes stock investors to sell off their holdings, the price might drop in three or four days an amount it took three or four weeks to build. However, if a position is held on a fundamentally sound stock, it will rise again if there is time to do so before expiration. Later, we'll look at a stock's cyclical pattern when we start reading charts.

> **Wise Option Traders Remember**
> *Be right and sit tight. Better to be pulled by knowledge than pushed by fear.*

Let's Talk about Greed

Greed can distort a trader's opportunity for success by bringing results similar to those brought about by fear. For example, you might think that you want just another $300 out of this option before you trade. Greed always pressures to get a little more. So, if you reach your $300 goal, then Greed shows up to whisper in your ear again, urging further gains until the stock drops with a natural adjustment in price.

All your life, someone, somewhere, has warned you about putting all your eggs in one basket. Well, here it is again. Greedy traders can get into trouble by putting too much money in too few option opportunities.

Why would a trader do this? Usually, the concentrated holdings result because she's looking for that "big trade," the big score. But this is a way to cut short a potentially great trading career.

Know Thyself

Above and beyond fear and greed, you also need to know yourself and your unique trading style. We all have distinct personalities, and trading styles and personalities differ, too. The way you trade must conform to your underlying personality.

- **Trader A.** For this trader, buying an option with an expiration date six months out might not be active enough to keep her interest. She quickly becomes bored with trading and she ends up drifting away before she's had a chance to reap the benefits.

- **Trader B.** This trader calls herself a *day trader,* meaning that she enters and exits options on the same day. This is another end of the spectrum of trading (and gets considerable attention because day traders have a reputation of being "on the edge" and in a frenzy as they chase after those hungry wolves). As a trading style, day trading demands constant attention to the market, and the trader must make decisions quickly in a short span of time. This quick pace trading can be exhilarating to some women and stressful to others.

Who Are You?

If you thrive on fast-paced action and are good at making speedy and frequent decisions, day trading might be a perfect fit. If, on the other hand, you're much more comfortable making carefully considered decisions, you wouldn't enjoy watching your fortunes changing hour by hour. For many of us, this would create unbearable stress.

On the other hand, as we said, a very slow pace might not keep your interest. For many, moderately *longer term position trading* fits best. Trading should feel comfortable and natural.

Although no two traders are exactly alike, this book presents and discusses universal trading principles that apply to all trading opportunities. Your comfortable trading personality—your trading posture—will likely reveal itself as you read through the material presented here and practice before you invest the first penny.

Understanding Risk

We discuss the issue of risk, and limiting risk, because it's closely linked to making good choices in selecting ripe, sound underlying stocks/ETFs/indexes. One basic way to reduce risk is by purchasing options on only the very best underlying instruments. Besides that, however, what potential risks must you consider?

Overall, options are less risky than stocks, because the amount that can be lost is limited and you know the amount the moment you choose to purchase an option.

Remember the all important characteristic of options–those who buy options limit their risk, but options have potentially unlimited reward.

Example

Let's say we decide to buy an option from the option chain below. (It is the same Wal-Mart chain shown earlier.) For this example, we'll purchase option WMTLW. This is:

- *December* option on *Wal-Mart* stock,

- when the stock price is *$48.21,*

- and a *strike price of $47.50,*

- which is $.71 in-the-money.

This option will cost us eighty cents (ask price–see chart below) per share (and since options are in lots of one hundred shares) the total will be $80 per contact. They are so inexpensive, let's make it worth while and buy three contracts, or three hundred shares, for a total of $240. This is the most that we can lose no matter what happens to the underlying stock. Wal-Mart stock can become worthless and what we have risked is $240 to control $14,463 of Wal-Mart stock.

WMT												48.21	+0.36
Wal-Mart Stores, Inc													

	Open:	47.82	High:	48.50
	Low:	47.80	Volume:	23,281,285
	Yield:	1.83%	P/E Ratio:	15.60
	Bid:	n/a	Ask:	n/a
	Ex Div. Date:	12/12/2007	Ex Div. Amount:	0.22

Pay $9.95. Get the works. | *charles* SCHWAB

OPTION CHAIN FOR WAL-MART STORES, INC

CALLS								PUTS					
Hide December, 2007 Options													
Symbol	Last	Change	Vol	Bid	Ask	Open Int.	StrikePrice	Symbol	Last	Change	Vol	Bid	Ask	Open Int.
WMTLG	13.20			13.20	13.30	32.00	35.00	WMTXG	0.05				0.05	6,510.00
WMTLU	10.70			10.70	10.80	54.00	37.50	WMTXU	0.05				0.05	4,712.00
WMTLH	8.40	+0.10	8.00	8.20	8.30	69.00	40.00	WMTXH	0.02				0.05	24,526.00
WMTLV	5.70	+0.40	131.00	5.70	5.80	393.00	42.50	WMTXV	0.03				0.05	16,819.00
WMTLI	3.19	+0.39	94.00	3.20	3.30	721.00	45.00	WMTXI	0.01				0.05	34,085.00
WMTLW	0.80	+0.40	3,948.00	0.70	0.80	45,354.00	47.50	WMTXW	0.05	-0.05	2,443.00		0.05	27,337.00
						Stock Price ▶	48.21	Last as of 12/21/2007 4:02:00 PM					
WMTLJ	0.05	+0.02	187.00		0.05	45,370.00	50.00	WMTXJ	1.75	-0.46	270.00	1.70	1.80	13,604.00
WMTLX	0.05				0.05	17,049.00	52.50	WMTXX	4.50	+0.20	10.00	4.20	4.40	161.00
WMTLK	0.05				0.05	7,838.00	55.00	WMTXK	6.85			6.70	6.90	15.00
WMTLY	0.05				0.05	7,730.00	57.50	WMTXY	10.10			9.20	9.40	22.00
WMTLL	0.05				0.05	4,524.00	60.00	WMTXL	11.80	-0.10	69.00	11.70	11.90	1.00
WMTLM	0.08				0.05	51.00	65.00	WMTXM	16.80	-0.10	69.00	16.60	16.90	71.00
WMTLN					0.05		70.00	WMTXN	21.80	-0.10	69.00	21.60	21.90	

When a stock increases or decreases in price it seldom does so in one fell swoop. It clicks up and down in penny/nickel/dime increments (obviously there are occasions when this happens quickly like the volatile market of late 2008 and 2009). At any point, if we decide that the market hasn't cooperated with our option choice, we can sell, cutting our loss short. In such a case, as in our example, the stock price of Wal-Mart drops ten cents to $48.11. In turn, our option has become less valuable. Maybe its value now is seventy-two cents each for the one hundred units of stock or $216 for our three contracts.

We have the choice of selling and taking a loss of $24, or holding on to the option because we bought out and have two months before expiration and our chart reading tells us this is just momentary profit taking by the big players and the stock is apt to continue its trend up.

Of course, part of our success strategy involves maximizing profit and to minimizing loss. We learn when to sell and walk away and when to hold because we have time and this is what our technical analysis tells us. Finally, we learn when to take profits off the table.

Another Risk Remedy

If you're worried that you will miss the market dropping (or rising in the case of a put) and leave you no time to get out of a position, there is a protective device in place for that–a safety net. This device allows you to set *stops* on your options, which will close the position if it drops below the point set.

Gaining Confidence

Learning how to trade options in a systematic way leads to confident investing, and confidence is a key to becoming empowered. We now see women of all ages, educational backgrounds, and locales joining this path to empowerment. We also see these women come to understand that they really are part of an elite group that involves taking controlled risks. They've left the image of investing as a roulette table or slot machine behind!

Most of us would agree that tightrope walkers or race-car drivers have risky occupations. But imagine a group of these acrobats or drivers getting together. Do you think they gulp down coffee and agonize about the risks they're taking? Not likely. These risks are no longer foremost in their minds. They have learned through techniques and skill how to minimize those risks. These individuals are much more likely to discuss a new tool that helps them perform even better, and they're likely to hang out with those who are successful.

By the time you finish this book and step on your trading path, you will see the opportunities and advantages of seeking other women option traders, either through our website, www.WomenOptionTraders.com, or through a face-to-face group in your community. Like the tightrope walkers and race-car drivers, you'll share the tools you've found to become successful, empowered option traders.

Chapter Three

WE BEGIN— CREATING YOUR PLAN

We've already discussed *underlying instruments,* which are types of investments or financial products. As you probably know, bookstore shelves are crammed with books that discuss the broad investing field and some address just one feature of it. For our purposes, we're focusing on three types of underlying instruments to trade—*Exchange Traded Funds (ETFs), indexes,* and *stocks.*

Exchange Traded Funds (ETFs)

ETFs are described as a collection of stocks that are bought and sold as a package on an exchange, principally the AMEX, but also NYSE, CBOE, and NASDAQ. In actuality, however, as a tool, ETFs offer more control than mutual funds and less risk than individual stocks. An ETF is a basket of stocks from a number of companies (which is what makes it similar to a mutual fund), representing various industries within a sector held by the ETF. This distinguishes it from stocks from an individual company. So, an ETF is like buying a basket of apples, oranges, pears, and so forth. They're different, but they're all fruit.

Right now, ETFs are in vogue, so to speak. Having come into their own as an investment instrument, new ETFs enter the marketplace every week. Some are optionable, while others are not. (*Optionable* simply means that options are offered for sale.) For example, a recently created ETF grouped cancer-related companies—pharmaceuticals, cancer care, hospitals, research, and hospice care.

ETFs bear the same code identification as stocks. For example:

- XAU–a group of stocks representing gold and silver;

- XLE–a group of stocks from the energy sector;

- UTH–Utilities Sector;

- SMH–Semiconductors;

- PPH–Pharmaceuticals;

- RTH–Retail;

- XLP–S&P Consumer Staples;

- IBB–NASDAQ Biotech.

Indexes

Many securities are traded on exchanges such as NASDAQ, AMEX, NYSE, and CBOE. You may be familiar with these exchanges because you hear the results of the day's activities on these exchanges on the financial reports. In addition, most daily newspapers list an abbreviated version of the results of the previous day's trading for one or more exchange.

An *index* is a group of stocks that are used as a measuring stick of sorts. The major indices, the Dow (Dow Jones Industrial Average), NASDAQ, S&P (Standard and Poor's), and Russell each list specific stocks unique to their index. Subsets of stocks within their lists create smaller indexes. For example, the S&P 100 is a smaller index listed within the S&P 500. Some of these indexes mimic the performance of their major index, while others are more sector-related.

We have an optionable index when groups of the top stocks combined within these indices are collected into an index with options available for trade.

Some of these are:

- QQQQ–called Qs, an index of the top one-hundred securities traded on the NASDAQ;

- DIA–called Diamonds, an index of the top twenty-five stocks traded on the Dow;

- SPY–called Spy or Spider, a group of securities traded on the Standard & Poor's index, the S&P 500; and,

- OEX–a group of one-hundred securities known as the S&P 100.

Why Purchase Options on Indexes or ETFs?

Indexes and ETFs are not subject to price fluctuations in the same way we see with an individual company. When an individual company reports an unexpected jump in quarterly earnings or an FDA approval for a drug is delayed, these events influence the stock one way or another. But with ETFs and indexes, up/down earning's reports, gains or losses of contracts, patents, FDA approval, indiscretions by the CEO, or other company successes or setbacks have little or no effect. Each company provides only one ripple within the large pond, and ETFs and indexes move with the industry, sector, or the market as a whole.

Indexes and ETFs are comprised of the relative weight of the whole group. One company can *falter*–drop in stock price–but its fortunes for the moment only minimally affect the ETF or Index. Of course, if a stock within the index is a major corporation like Apple or Google, the index may drop a bit, but not to the degree experienced by the stock itself. This means that ETF or index options carry less risk than options on an individual company.

If we must put a negative twist on ETFs and indexes, then we'd have to say that because the risk level is less, the level of reward is proportionate. These instruments plod along on surer footing, moving up and down in relatively small increments, and without the mood swings we see with some individual stocks. For those who want less risky option opportunities, ETFs and indexes are the ideal way to go.

Why Purchase Stock Options?

Stock available in individual companies is a distinct and divisible part of the market whole. Newly listed companies on the market seem to express themselves with youthful exuberance, experiencing their greatest physical growth in their early years. Later in life it's only their weight that grows.

Often these young, restless companies rise to prominence because they offer a new and innovative product or service that quickly grabs interest and a large following. Some of the biggest market winners tend to notch their way to gains in the first eight years (on average) following their *initial public offering* (IPO).

During the figure-conscious days of a young company, it often draws the attention of major investors, generally the institutional investors, who are attracted to the most dramatic stages of the company's development, the sharp sales growth, reliability, and earnings growth. As firms mature, their growth tends to slow. The numbers that made one-year-ago comparisons easy and exciting become harder to sustain. Eventually, these companies are like older people! They may be elegant and strong and accorded respect, but they no longer inspire adrenalin rushes in the hungry wolf packs in the investing world. In some cases, they seem to do little more than plod along.

Today, General Electric (GE) is one of the older companies with sound fundamentals. It doesn't offer the excitement of say, First Solar (FSLR), which designs, manufactures, and sells solar electric power modules. Likewise, IBM (IBM) is one of the players that ushered us into the information age, but EMC Corporation (EMC) engages in the development, delivery, and support of the information infrastructure technologies and solutions worldwide.

In a worst case scenario, some tried and true companies may grow complacent and fall into mismanagement. Sometimes they are able to remake themselves, as, for example, Ford Motor Company (F) is attempting to do. They hope to start a new long-term advance with reinvigorated drive and spirit.

If it hadn't been for some long-term creative thinking, Apple (AAPL), the maker of the popular Macintosh computers, might have landed in this complacent category. However, in recent years Apple stayed prominent with its iPod digital music players, and then in 2007, it unveiled the iPhone, hoping to nab even more consumers.

In some ways, Apple could be viewed as an eccentric rogue neighbor, who will likely shock and surprise you from time to time.

A Critical Tool for a Successful Trading Plan

One of the critical steps to profitable trading is finding and regularly consulting a reliable source of stock (and ETF) candidates. The easiest, most direct route to that information is the *Investors Business Daily* (IBD), the newspaper that is the stock and option traders' bible. You may subscribe and receive the newspaper through the mail or pick one up at newsstands.

Subscribers to the IBD also have full access to its Internet site, www.Investors.com. All of the information listed in the paper is available online. You'll see that we've included a clip from the paper showing a sample of the information we can use to our advantage. In addition, our website, www.WomenOptionTraders.com, provides a link to an undated listing of the top IBD one hundred stocks, along with their current price charts.

We encourage you to avail yourself of these charts, but nothing is better than the hands-on experience of locating, documenting, and creating a list of these potential option trade candidates. By doing so, you'll become familiar with and recognize symbols, patterns, prices, as well as recent history.

IBD Composite Rating
Earnings Per Share Growth Rating
Relative Price Strength Rating
Sales+Profit Margins+Return On Equity
Accumulation/Distribution [Last 3 mos]

52-wk High	Stock	Dividend % Yield	Symbl	Close Price	Chg	Vol% Chg	Vol 1000	P E

Common stocks above $10 for Friday, September 12, 2008

1. MEDICAL

99	99	93	A B	77.4	Celgene	CELG ●	71.15	+.48	–8	4.3m	53o
54	69	21	B D	–40.0	Abaxis	ABAX	19.48	+.46	–49	200	36o
94	77	85	A B	+61.1	AbbotLa	2.4 ABT	59.09	–.22	–6	6.5m	19o
63	6	92	E C	+20.1	Abiomed	ABMD	17.45	–.34	–21	280	..o
85	47	96	C C	+79.0	AbraxisBn	ABII	74.08	+1.10	–15	24	99
59	3	95	E D	+35.7	AcordaTh	ACOR	27.51	+.48	–43	448	..o
56	52	67	D B	–32.1	AdvMOpt	EYE	22.46	–.12	–49	477	99o
80	86	48	B B	60.0	Aetna	.1 r AET	42.52	–.46	–42	2.8m	11o
46	1	81	D D	–32.0	Affymax	AFFY	19.97	–.04	–45	28	..
46	42	20	B C	+59.5	AirMethods	AIRM	28.10	+.21	–42	152	16o
93	55	96	D B	+19.1	AlbanyMlc	AMRI	18.00	–.57	–19	172	48o
99	91	89	A B	176	►Alcon	1.5 ACL ●	169.1	+.63	+30	453	28o
92	73	95	E D	+48.0	AlexionPhr	ALXN	41.53	–.48	–55	769	..o
60	7	73	C B	–18.8	Alkermes	r ALKS	12.99	–.33	–35	1.0m	46
96	82	73	A B	70.4	Allergan	.3 AGN	59.74	–.79	+91	4.6m	25o
79	32	96	.. A	–12.0	Alliancimg	AIQ	11.67	–.13	–59	102	38
99	95	99	A B	46.5	AlmstFam	AFAM	41.98	+1.68	–24	264	25
81	54	81	D C	+37.4	AlnylamPh	ALNY	28.62	+.35	–49	282	..
82	40	99	D A	–NH	Alphrma	r ALO	37.75	+.37	+142	3.9m	99o
99	93	87	A C	68.0	Amedisys	AMED ●	48.15	–.35	–28	992	17o
81	73	96	E B	13.2	AmerSvcGp	r ASGR	10.91	–.08	–46	42	99
97	83	91	C B	+18.6	AmMedSys	AMMD	17.34	–.10	–43	544	30o
67	78	47	B C	+41.0	Amerigrp	AGP	25.61	–.70	–6	655	9o
77	78	70	C B	–48.6	AmeriBrg	.7 r ABC	41.07	+.24	+1	1.6m	14o

Chart appears courtesy of Investors.com

What Should You Look for in the Newspaper or Online?

No matter how you slice or dice it, choosing great underlying stocks is arguably the most important mechanical aspect of a successful trading plan. Having a pool of high-quality potential trade candidates is like having a stocked pantry with all the staples. All the tools of the trading plan are useless without a consistent source of the basic ingredients to choose from.

Another reason this is critical is that relying on a consistent source of high quality trade candidates saves you from the need to turn to hunches, tips, or the conflicting opinions of TV analysts. The stock-tip industry is big business and TV analysts and other financial journalists may point out companies with an interesting story. But do they have agendas of their own?

Most TV analysts live either in the bull or bear camp, and they'd certainly love to have their predictions validated by accurately foretelling the market's future or a stock's price movement–and in front of millions of viewers no less.

While not all of these analysts are employed by brokerage houses, most are, and they and their brokerage firms are selling their services. In addition, many of these analysts privately sell stock-tip newsletters or tip services for a healthy fee. This doesn't make these individuals wrong or unethical, but they are part of the big picture of not only trading itself, but of the huge financial advisory business.

We've certainly heard enough stories to know that you can go broke chasing tips. A feature in a magazine or on TV with a title like *Ten Options You Simply Must Buy,* or other similar stories, usually fail to mention market conditions, technical analysis, or any clue as to when to buy, when to sell, or where to stop if all goes wrong.

On the other hand, when you do your own research, you're treating your trading like a business, and you're basing your decisions on sound principles, learned techniques, and choosing financially sound trade candidates with the highest fundamentals. In order to identify a consistent flow of great stocks on which to purchase options, we will sift them through a sieve to see which ones hold up and make the grade.

What Do You See?

Using the IBD–either the hard-copy newspaper or their online site–open the paper to *Section B* or find the NYSE (New York Stock Exchange) and NASDAQ Research Tables on the IBD site. Though there are interesting articles, opinions, and other information throughout the pages, we are going to concern ourselves with information that we analyze, thus becoming the experts of our own plan. We'll go through the stock tables item by item, step by step.

Wise Option Traders Remember
A favorite restaurant chain doesn't guarantee success, and well-known stocks don't always succeed.

The NYSE and NASDAQ Research Tables list all the New York Stock Exchange companies and NASDAQ with stocks priced at $10 and above. From the information in this newspaper or online column, plus using the parameters given below, you can form a list.

Across the top of the first column you will see listed from left to right: *IBD Composite Rating, Earnings Per Share Growth Rating, Relative Price Strength Rating, Sales + Profit Margins + Return on Equity, Accumulation/ Distribution (last 3 months), 52-Week High,* and so on. You'll find a wealth of information concisely packed in these two-inch columns.

We will focus on the *Earnings Per Share, Relative Price Strength* and *Industry Sector* and also the column to the right of *Accumulation/Distribution,* listed as *52-Week High.*

Until early 2008, the IBD listed stocks only in alphabetical order, but in March of that year they began categorizing stocks by industry sector and highlighting the few stocks with the best recent price action, while leaving the rest of the sector's stocks in an alphabetical list. This means that thirty-two industry sectors are listed in the order of *daily performance strength.*

This change provides a great service to investors. For example, if the Medical sector's performance places them as number one, it makes sense to evaluate those stocks more closely than Energy sector stocks whose perfor-mance may put them at twenty-eight.

When you first begin to create a list, many candidates will survive the ever-decreasing criteria, but as you check future papers you'll find fewer acceptable stocks, yet a few will improve their standing and rise to be noticed.

- **Step 1.** Scan the *closing price* column on the middle right. If the price is $25 or more move to Step 2.

  □ *Explanation.* There are certainly sound stocks with prices under $25, but as option traders we want to concentrate on purchasing options on stocks that realize fast-growing returns.

The profit on a $25 stock will be proportionally greater than profit on a $10 stock. Low-priced stocks are risky, because they usually have low trading volume. It is hard for big institutional investors to buy shares without causing a major mood swing in the share price.

- **Step 2.** Now look to the farthest right section of the column for a small *o or o/k*. The presence of an *o* means the stock is *optionable,* so you can go on to Step 3. If there is no *o*, options are not available on this stock. (The *k* means that earnings are due to be announced within four weeks.)

> **Wise Option Traders Remember**
> *Cheap stocks are cheap for a reason.*

- **Step 3.** Once you have an optionable stock priced over $25, scan over to the left of the company name to *EPS (Earnings per Share)*. We are looking for a number higher than 80. If the number is lower move on to the next $25 candidate that is optionable. 80 +

  □ *Explanation.* Wall Street rewards performance. Nowhere is that more true than when it comes to a firm's earnings results. Studies of the greatest market winners have found that earnings growth has the biggest impact on a stock's price performance. Whether a company sells hamburgers, panty hose, or jet engines, its goal is always the same–*increase the bottom line.* A stock with an EPS rating of eighty means the company is outperforming most or many of the other firms in terms of quarterly and annual profit growth. IBD uses a scale of one (worst) to ninety-nine (best) to signify the composite of these EPS results.

- **Step 4.** The column to the right of EPS is *Relative Price Strength* (RS). A number better than ninety is what is needed in order to continue through our sieve. 90 +

  □ *Explanation.* Buying a stock is like buying a piece of fruit. You want it to be fresh, in good shape, ripening nicely, and sweet. In stock terms that means the stock has a good uptrend, is in a good price movement pattern, and is profitable. High quality stock comes at a premium. But like most things in life, you get what you pay for.

Relative Strength is a measure of a stock's price performance compared to an index or a huge basket of other stocks. It's basically a measuring tool to use to judge how stocks have performed relative to the market or segments of the market. For example, it may sound great to hear a TV analyst say that a stock went up 10% last month, but if the stock market as a whole rose 10%, then the stock's performance was in line. But we want stocks that not only hang around with the majority of the market, but also outperform it. So, an RS rating of ninety-nine tells you that the stock has outperformed 99% of all the stocks in IBD's database over the last twelve months. Stocks with RS Ratings of ninety or below tend to lag the overall market.

Wise Option Traders Remember
The goal: buy high, sell higher.

Run through the entire list using this criteria.

What Made the First Cut?

If a stock passes all four sifting screens, we have a candidate to track; we follow it to learn when it is ripe to purchase its options. List your candidates in a notebook, noting name, stock symbol, and stock price. As we move into technical analysis, you will put this list to use.

Before we move on, let's look at two other bits of information.

• Look at the IBD newspaper column entry, *52-Week High,* and if you see an *NH* (New High), note this by writing an NH next to the price. This New High price will correspond to that stock's price.

   □ Explanation. If we are focusing on stocks that have hit their 52-week high, we are zeroing in on stocks that have already proved themselves. Such stocks have high valuations for a simple reason: investors think they're worth it. Since these stocks are pushing into new territory, they don't have to contend with *overhead resistance,* a concept we discuss in detail in a later chapter.

• For our last notation on our list of candidates, find the column with heading *Accumulation/Distribution.* A hallmark of a great stock is that there are more buyers than sellers. The Accumulation/Distribution rating gauges that buying power. Strong accumulation is a sign that the biggest investors, (i.e., mutual funds, insurance companies, and other institutions) are buying the stock.

Accumulation/Distribution ratings appear as a letter grade.

- A–heavy buying
- B–moderate
- C–equal weight
- D–moderate selling
- E–heavy selling

C or better (handwritten)

The system gives the greatest weight to the most recent 13-week period, reflecting and emphasizing the stock's most recent history.

This letter grade is particularly important as a stock retreats in price. Of course, that price retreat can be a natural part of growth, like stopping to take a deep breath before another burst of speed. However, if its rating drops it could be a sign that big investors are dumping large amounts of the stock.

Note: Institutional investors–usually shortened to *tutes*–including mutual funds, pension funds, banks, and so forth, command the majority of the action in the market. As our packs of wolves hunt through the woods, they have the speed and appetite to run stocks up and then drop them even faster when they believe they're spoiled or at least are no longer fresh. That's the reason we monitor their actions. It's critical to track the tutes!

For our candidates, let's require a report card of *C* or better, making a note of it in our notebook. Then as we check the stock technically we can look back on this grade. For example, if it falls two full notches, say, from B to D, that's a possible signal it's not a time to buy, or it could be a sell signal.

So, we now have a list of stock candidates as well as optionable ETFs and indexes. We can narrow the search further for companies worthy of purchasing an option today or next week.

Chapter Four

CHART READING 101

For many women, this stage, chart reading–the nitty-gritty of learning to trade–is also a stage that may trigger fear, at least to some degree. Specifically, I've noticed that too many women become fearful about messing up. They usually feel this way because all the pieces of this particular puzzle aren't in place yet. Even so, most women have become programmed to expect a great deal from themselves, even instant under-standing and immediate perfection. These high expectations can lead to the fear of making a mistake.

But, if you're afraid to make a mistake, you're destined to interfere with the process that will ultimately make you a successful trader. Blame it on conditioning or the pressure so many women feel to do it all, it seems this is a tough lesson for many women. Yet, far from being the end of the world, mistakes are your ticket to new understanding.

Not long ago, my ten-year-old granddaughter Lauren stayed overnight with me, and when she got into bed, I sat with her so we could have a good talk before saying good night. She's at a great age, a time when she's primed to receive information that will help her build a strong and powerful self-image.

I asked her to tell me about something that used to be hard for her to do, but is easy now.

"Cheerleading," she immediately said, followed by riding a bike.

I kept prompting her to think of more things, and we got to writing and making pancakes.

It was fun to watch her eyes widen in wonder when I told her all the things she learned that she couldn't remember–rolling over, sitting up, crawling, walking, talking, holding a fork, making her bed, and on and on. I told her how each of those things had been hard for her in the beginning. She's struggled and made mistakes, yet she can do all of them easily, without giving them much thought. Because she's still a child, Lauren can accept that the same rules apply to all the new things she's learning. She's open to the idea that mistakes are teachers. It's as simple as that. Unlike so many adults, she doesn't spend much time complaining and whining about mistakes either!

So, don't fear mistakes. Use them as feedback. Mistakes lead to greatness, but only if we stop judging them as negative. By the end of these next chapters you will be able to read and interpret charts. You'll be able to practice trading without actually losing a dime. Some of your choices will be winners and some losers, but each choice will be a teacher, putting you on the path to financial empowerment.

Back to Your List and IBD *next*

Based on your work in the last chapter, you now have a list of stock candidates. Now it's time to zero in on the *stock sectors* that are in favor. Sectors are a bit like specialty stores that carry goods from many manufacturers. A rule of thumb is that a sector's standing and movement accounts for 50% of an individual stock's movement. Once you know which sectors are making gains, you can narrow your focus to specific stocks in those sectors.

On the first day you scanned the IBD for candidates your list started with those in the leading sectors, but as time passes sectors shift positions as a new sector begins to out-perform the rest. So to find the current leading sector, you go back to the IBD—the source of so much information. As your list becomes dated, scan it for candidates that fall into the current top rated sectors.

Below is a consolidated list of stock sectors you'll be studying and working with. Two of the eleven sectors listed below are considered to be *defensive,* meaning they don't always fall when the market drops, thus they provide a soft landing. This is the case because, no matter what, people don't stop using energy or eating or needing toilet paper. However, for all their safe qualities, these sectors usually fail to climb at a fast rate in a rising market. Their protection becomes their limitation, because a rising market doesn't mean that people use appreciably more of the necessities.

The other nine sectors are *cyclical,* meaning they rotate in and out of favor, based on the time of the year or market conditions.

IBD's broad list of thirty-two sectors each fall within this consolidated list. For example, IBD's bank, insurance, finance, and savings and loan sectors all fit into the broad financial sector.

- *Defensive Sectors*

  □ Utilities

  □ Consumer Staples

- *Cyclical Sectors*

  □ Basic Materials

  □ Capital Goods

  □ Consumer Cyclical

  □ Energy

  □ Communications

  □ Healthcare

  □ Technology

  □ Financial

  □ Transportation

Another method of checking sector movement is to see which stocks are making new highs. IBD lists the number of companies within a sector hitting new highs and lows.

In addition, IBD also lists and ranks 197 industries within those sectors, so we are able to become even more specific in our choices. For example, within the Energy sector, there are companies involved with machinery and equipment, drilling, transportation and pipelines, exploration, and so forth. Each industry within the Energy sector has its own ranking each week.

Why is this important? When you're picking the ripe stocks, you will know that it doesn't make sense to consider Wal-Mart or Best Buy, for example, as option candidates if retail companies are in an early summer sales slump, as opposed to the holiday season or back-to-school months, which are typically better times for retail.

Perhaps, you begin examining stocks during a period that other sectors, such as telecom, agriculture, or technology are in favor. Again, IBD's top sector list of companies reaching new highs and industry rankings will help pinpoint where to concentrate your search.

Earlier in our discussion on sectors, we noted as an example that the Medical sector was number one. Under the newspaper heading *IBD's 197 Industry Sub Group Rankings,* we could find that the industry subgroup Medical–Genetics was listed as the number one. Medical Outpatient and Homecare was six, Medical/Dental–Services was eight, Medical Products was seventeen, Medical–Generic Drugs was eighteen, and Medical–Systems/Equipment was nineteen. In this example, we would locate within our candidate list stocks that fall within the leading sectors (maybe the top six sectors) and then narrow further to those within the highest ranking industry sub-groups within those sectors.

Here's a real life example. In November of 2006, Wendy concentrated her search on the pharmaceutical industry, purchasing options on companies such as WellCare Group (WCG), Prudential Insurance (PRU), and LHC Group (LHCG). These stocks advanced and her options profited until April of 2007, when the cycle began to change. She sold and scouted out the next hot sector and rotated her investing funds into the Energy sector, knowing if a storm occurred as the summer driving and hurricane season approached, oil drilling and supply might be interrupted in the Gulf of Mexico. In addition, at that time an increased demand for air conditioning would be underway.

Wendy purchased options on Oceaneering Intl., Inc. (OII), Transocean (RIG), and Dry Ships, Inc. (DRYS), a company that transports commodities like coal and iron ore. In addition, she bought options on solar stocks, knowing as other energy sources rose in cost, solar stocks would become more popular and profitable. SunPower Corp. (SPWR) and FLIR Systems, Inc. (FLIR) steadily climbed during the next six months to burst to new heights on huge volume in October and November of 2007.

Note: We wrote this book to provide readers with a basic foundation of information about option trading, and we've provided sample charts and other examples to illustrate our points. However, these examples are not meant to be viewed as stock or option recommendations or endorsements of individual companies.

Checking for Ripeness with *Technical Screens*

Once you have narrowed down your sector or industry candidates, you'll run them through technical screens to check for ripeness. These *technical indicators* show where the stock is in its market cycle, and they explain what the graph says about its price.

After we explain the individual indicators, we will put it all together, step by step. Here are some facts to remember:

- In addition to giving a picture of an individual stock, stock charts contain an abundance of information about what is happening in the overall market.

- Charts can be set up for a number of different time periods–daily, weekly, monthly, yearly, and even shorter periods of time, including hourly and minute-by-minute.

- Each chart creates a picture of the stock's position within the market as a whole and where it stands in its own life cycle.

Information that can be derived from the chart below includes the following:

- Daily highs and lows

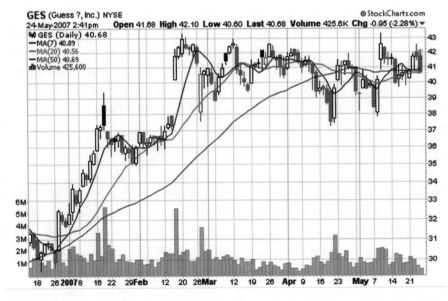

Chart courtesy of StockCharts.com

• Open and closing prices

• Volume

• Six-months trading average

• Buying pressure and selling pressure

The information across the top of the chart tells you which company, ETF, or index this chart refers to. In this case, it's Guess, Inc., a clothing company. You can follow the data from left to right and see that the upper area also shows the date, the open, high, low, and closing price, volume and the change in dollars and percent that amount represents of a stock's total price.

Below this bar to the left tells you that this is a daily chart and it repeats the closing price.

Information about time runs horizontally from left to right at the bottom of the chart, with the left being the furthest in the past, right being the most recent.

This chart indicates that we're looking at a six month chart covering the clothing company's price history over that period of time. The price scale is displayed on the right side of the chart. As we move our eye from right to left, we are moving from the most recent price information and journeying into the past. The bottom of the main chart shows volume; usually two bars of different colors.

Looking at the Candlesticks

We need to understand the *candlestick,* or *candle,* which is an important technical symbol on charts in general. You will see them on your computer in red, black, and hollow. Candlesticks provide information about the *average* price of the underlying stock. They reflect the price action over the course of the market session.

Note: When you look at the charts printed on these pages, you'll notice that some mention colors that indicate lines and other symbols on the chart. Since the charts in this book are printed in black and white, we have developed guidelines to help you read and interpret the chart.

Candlesticks on charts are generally shown as solid and in one of two colors, black and red, or as hollow. On the charts that follow, the darkest shading indicates *black* and the gray shading indicates *red.*

Trend lines or channels are shown as blue lines, but you will see them here as straight, unbroken lines.

Moving averages (MAs) generally are shown in blue for 7-day MA, red for 20-day MA, and green for 50-day MA. (The MA code appears on the upper left corner of the chart.) In this book, you will see three degrees of shading:

Darkest=7-day MA
Lightest=20-day MA
Medium shading=50-day MA

(You may prefer to view the charts at our website, www.WomenOption Traders.com, in order to match the text with the color-coded chart. We have posted *every* stock and index symbol shown in this book—and many more. Simply click on the blog tab, open the blog, and go to the *Public Charts* link on the right side.)

- If it is a daily chart, the candle reflects the movement that day from opening to closing bell.

- If the chart is a weekly chart, then the candle reflects an accumulation of the week's activity through that week. The last candlestick (on the right) can be a partial if you are viewing it before the closing bell or week's end. Those, too, are usually two colors, often red and black and are either solid or hollow (unfilled). The thin, long lines above and below the body of the candle represent the high/ low range of the session, and are called *shadows* (or sometimes they are referred to as *wicks* and *tails*). The relationship between the opening and closing price is vital information and forms the essence of candlestick symbols.

- Hollow candlesticks, where the close price is *greater* than the open price, indicate *buying* pressure.

• Filled candlesticks, where the close price is *less* than the open price (usually red), indicates *selling* pressure.

The candlestick's color and position on the chart will reflect:

• whether the price closed higher or lower than the price at the opening of the day; and,

• where it closed in comparison to the previous periods.

Generally speaking, the *longer* the body of the candlestick, the more *intense* the buying and selling pressure.

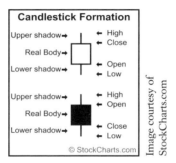

Conversely, *short* candlestick bodies indicate *little* price movement and represents consolidation.

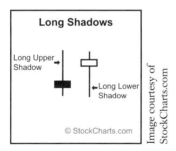

First, note where the solid candle opened and closed in relation to the high and low of the period. What does this relationship tell us?

It indicates that there was a great deal of (bullish) positive buying interest, which was barely overcome by the (bearish) downward momentum selling. How do we know this? Look how far the stock price went up after the market opened (represented by the topmost shadow or wick). Note, too, how little the downside was by comparison. Even though this reflects a down day for this stock, the size of the candle's body shows little selling (bearish) strength.

Conversely, hollow candlesticks with long lower shadows and short upper shadows or wicks indicate that sellers dominated during the session and drove prices lower. However, buyers later rallied to bid prices higher by the end of the session and the strong close into positive territory created a long lower shadow.

Additionally, the shape and size of the candle tells us a great deal more. A candlestick depicts a football game between the buyers (Bulls) and the sellers (Bears). The bottom of the candlestick (the session's low) represents the Bears' goal-line and the top is the Bulls' goal-line. The closer the close to the low, the closer the Bears are to a touchdown. The closer the close to the high, the closer the Bulls are to a touchdown. The various shapes and sizes of the candlesticks indicate who controlled the ball for most of the game period.

Now consider the candlesticks in the figure below. What can we infer? Who ruled the day? Bulls' buying was very strong, with very little selling.

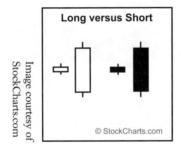

Image courtesy of StockCharts.com

- Long, hollow candles, with "shortish" shadows show strong buying pressure.

- Long red candles show strong selling pressure. The longer the body, the more intense the buying or selling pressure.

- Conversely, short candlesticks indicate little price movement and represent consolidation.

Even more potent candlesticks are those with no shadows (as seen below), called *Marubozu.*

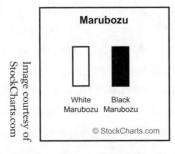

Image courtesy of StockCharts.com

This happens to a hollow candlestick when the opening price equals the low price and the closing equals the high. This shows that *buyers* controlled the price action from the first sale to the last trade of the period.

Charts using red candlesticks depicting a black Marubozu with no shadows form when the open price equals the high of the period and the closing price equals the low of the period. This indicates that sellers controlled the price action from the first trade to the last trade of the period.

Though much information can be gleaned from candlestick symbols, they don't represent the sequence of events between the open and close, only the ending relationship between the open and close. The high and low are obvious, but the candlesticks cannot tell us which came first. That means that this particular information doesn't mean as much in our decision to purchase an option as information about where the stock closed at the end of the period.

Wise Option Traders Remember
When a candlestick closes in the upper two-thirds, a large number of institutions have bought and are showing interest.

Other candlestick configurations involve size and lengths of shadows and their relationship to other candlesticks, and these add to our stock chart reading and help us predict what to expect. We cover these in a glossary of definitions at the end of the book.

Trend Trading–Examining Trends

Next, we examine the *trend line,* a simple and useful technical tool. Literally, this line is drawn along the trend of a stock's price over time. Until we delve deeper into creating our own charts this trend line can be one drawn by the eye or by holding up a small piece of paper or business card under the lower portions of the candles.

We are first and foremost trend traders. The trend is an accurate view of a stock's value whether real or perceived. We generally do not trade options against the trend. If a stock is in an uptrend, we consider buying calls. If a stock is in a downtrend, we consider purchasing puts.

The upward inclining line depicts a strong uptrend, and using that trend, we would purchase and hold call options (if our other screens have indicated that it is ripe). As you can see in the next figure, WCG's stock trended up from December through April 23. The profit potential in a trending stock such as this is staggering. It is very clear on this chart that your potential for trading success would be enhanced by following the trend rather than swimming against the current.

Examining Channels

Stock prices often reside within high and low limits. This pattern can be very evident on a chart. To draw a channel simply draw or imagine a trend line along the lows of the candlesticks as shown in this figure. Then draw a second line along the tops of the candlesticks. These two trend lines form a channel. Imagine now how it seems as if the candle hits the upper trend line like an invisible ceiling. Then it drops down only to bounce trampoline style off an imaginary floor.

The floor is called *support* and the overhead ceiling is called *resistance*. The support reflects the supply of this stock and resistance reflects demand. You can easily think and remember this by thinking about gravity and the support needed to hold things up. Resistance is a barrier that prevents or inhibits something from going higher. (We'll discuss other types of support and resistance lines later.)

So, these are the two most important principles involved in understanding chart analysis, and subsequently profitable trading.

1. *Support* is a price level to which prices tend to descend but not break through.

WCG (WellCare Group, Inc.) NYSE — StockCharts.com
24-May-2007 3:39pm   Open 90.76 High 92.65 Low 90.56 Last 90.96 Volume 778.9K Chg +0.20 (+0.22%)
WCG (Daily) 90.96
MA(7) 90.12
MA(20) 87.22
MA(50) 88.42
Volume 778,863

Solid, Straight Lines Indicate Channel

Chart courtesy of StockCharts.com

2. *Resistance* is a price level to which prices tend to ascend but not pass through.

The key word here is *tend.* These imagined lines of floors and ceilings hold through most price movement whether it is daily, weekly, monthly or yearly activity. It takes something out of the ordinary to happen to break through the support and resistance lines. These could include reporting triple earnings growth or a large loss, a major lawsuit against the company, an overall stock market reversal, FDA refused drug approval, or the end of an extended up/down trend.

Support and resistance lines gain strength as the time frame lengthens. For example, support and resistance lines in a sixty-minute chart might hold for a few days; in a daily chart they might remain unbreakable for a number of weeks; a monthly chart's lines might be steadfast for years.

If we looked at newspaper articles or financial journal reports, we could discover what rocked WCG on April 25 in the chart above, thus causing it to break through its support line. Then, on May 7, only a few weeks later, WCG shot back up and almost fully recovered after reporting stellar earnings.

As noted in the next charts, channels may be horizontal, upward, or downward. By watching for levels of support and resistance we will find natural trade entry and exit points. We would consider purchasing an option when a stock starts to come up off the support floor, holding through the body of the channel. We then watch closely, being ready to sell as the stock's price comes close to the ceiling resistance and if our purchased option is approaching its expiration date. While it's possible that the stock might break through resistance to then go higher, we will stand ready to sell in case the stock doesn't have the thrust-power to do so. In other words, we'll be ready to sell once the stock hits resistance, thus likely to descend back toward support.

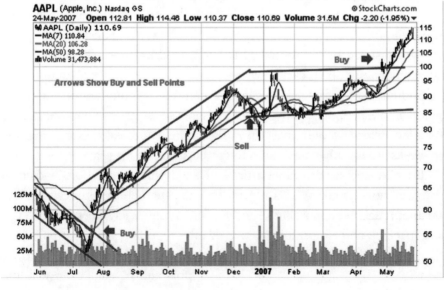

Chart courtesy of StockCharts.com

Other Indicators

We can use other indicators to help anticipate a change in a stock's direction before it happens.

- When a stock's price breaks out of a downward or horizontal channel with increased volume or other confirming indicators (heading upward), it is a possible trade signal.

- Volume is another crumb that the institutional buyers leave for us to follow, indicating the direction they have gone. Volume is often heavy when things are about to change, signaling a breakout of support or resistance, and a possible change in trend.

- When a stock's price breaks support, dropping out of an upward channel, it is a possible sell signal. This breakout and all other technical indicators are considered, along with general market conditions and harmony–agreement–with the stock's associated sector, and then we decide what action to take.

When trading a new uptrend or upside breakout, we go *long,* meaning we buy call options with the move out of the channel on higher volume. If the price drops back into the channel, then we immediately sell the position. Channel breakouts occur in either direction, up or down. (We discuss the down trend breakout in our chapter on puts.)

We also need to watch and consider support and resistance lines once we've purchased an option. For example, if we'd bought an option on a stock at its rock bottom price, close to its support line (the bottom of the channel), then we watch it closely as it rises to the first line of resistance. We're paying close attention to see if the stock will go on to break through or whether it is time to sell and take profits, because once it hits this ceiling it's apt to drop back down within the channel.

So, as you can see, we're watching activity taking place between the lines of support and resistance.

- At *support,* our crazed pack of stock buyers think, "What a bargain! I think I'll buy some stock at this low price."

- At *resistance,* buyers begin to lose confidence and are no longer inclined to make stock purchases. Here, sellers begin to take profit, decreasing demand, and driving the price back down.

- Then, with the price low, the buyers step back in, ready to purchase what again seems to be an abundant supply at bargain prices, and that drives the prices back up.

This dance of two-stepping–a number of steps up and a couple steps back, or a number of steps down and a couple steps up–continues until the price of the underlying security breaks through resistance. Then, that old line of resistance becomes a line of support for the next leg up. Or, if the price drops through support, then that old support line becomes a new line of resistance for the next leg up.

Technical analysis is not an exact science, so we can never totally predict what is going to happen. That's why it's important to be aware of these lines and vigilant when the underlying security gets near support and resistance. Our goal is to have time to react and avoid being caught unaware by a huge price move.

Simple Moving Averages (SMAs)

Another type of line of support and resistance lies with *moving averages*. When we create a chart, we have the choice of where to set the *Simple Moving Average* (SMAs). For our purposes in this book, we most often reference the 7-day, 20-day, or 50-day SMAs, and other at times the 40-day. (In its charts, the IBD most often uses a 10-week line, which corresponds to our 50-day (5 days x 10 weeks = 50 days).

In the left hand corner of a chart, the notation will tell you which type of moving averages (MAs) are used and the price that moving average reached.

If a security is trading above any of the moving averages that are incorporated within the chart, watch what happens when the price reaches the support of the SMA. Likewise, if it is trading below, watch what happens when it reaches the resistance of the SMA.

Notice the SMA lines that have been added to Apple's (AAPL) three-month candlestick chart. These lines add additional information for our consideration. The lines become areas of support and resistance. Ideally, in an uptrend, we want the 7-day SMA to be on top of the 20-day SMA and those two to be on top of the 50-day SMA. This strong uptrending pattern is shown on the chart from April 26 through May.

AAPL (Apple, Inc.) Nasdaq GS
24-May-2007 **Open** 112.81 **High** 114.46 **Low** 110.37 **Close** 110.69 **Volume** 31.5M **Chg** -2.20 (-1.95%) ▾
⓴ AAPL (Daily) 110.69
─MA(7) 110.84
─MA(20) 106.28
─MA(50) 98.28
▥ Volume 31,488,414

Black = 7-day MA
Lightest Gray = 20-day MA
Med Gray = 50-day MA

Chart courtesy of StockCharts.com

Note: To calculate a moving average, a 20-day SMA of price, for example, add the closing prices of twenty consecutive candles. Then divide this sum by twenty. This product is the price point, which is marked on the chart. On the following day, the previous twentieth day is dropped from the total and the new day one is added. This calculation is made again and again and plotted. Charting software then connects these plotted points with a smooth line.

Moving averages help to illuminate the current price positions as compared with the recent past. When we advance to creating our own charts, you will be able to choose how broad a view you'd like by selecting the number of calculation periods used in the construction of the moving averages. The determination of how many moving average periods to employ is based primarily on the expected duration of the option. If you are planning to be in an option for 1–6 weeks for example, a 30- to 50-day moving average would be useful in determining the current trend. One can easily understand that a 100-day SMA would be too long and a 5-day would be too short to give a good picture of a stock's trend.

Notice that the shorter the periods used for calculating the average, the closer the line will follow the up and down movement of the candlesticks. In the case of AAPL's chart above, the 7-day moving average rides right underneath the line of candles. If you look more closely, during an uptrend the candles are on top of the line. In a sideways movement, the line cuts through the candles, and during a downward trend, the candles drop below the line.

From July 23 through August 27, in the middle of the time line, Buffalo Wild Wings' price is below the SMAs and they are in reverse order with the blue on the bottom, red in the middle and green on top. This lineup corresponds to down trending movement.

Notice how the SMA lines act as resistance. It took from July 23 to mid-September for a price candle to have the momentum (buying volume) to break above these lines of resistance. It made an attempt to break through these SMAs on August 16, but there was enough selling pressure on August 22 that the price couldn't hold and it dropped back below through the lines of resistance that for only a few days had become lines of support. Again, on September 18, the bulls (buying pressure) attempted to break through resistance. This break only fully happened on September 27, as the SMAs lined up again with the 7-day on top, thus starting a new uptrend.

The Bears challenged again on October 9. On that day, selling pressure (the Bears) pushed the price downward, and for the next five days the price dropped. When the candles hit support at the 20-day moving average, it fought to maintain its position there. It then went into a period of consolidation (equal buying and selling) as shown by the four candles along the $39 price mark.

Trade signals are made in the direction of the shortest moving average (in our case, 7-day) as it crosses the longer time frame moving average (20-day and then 50-day).

Piercing up is a buy signal and piercing down is a sell signal. Now, if we had purchased an option contract on September 20, as the candle closed above the 20-day SMA (or the surer signal on September 27, when the candle closed above the 7-day SMA), and as the 7-day SMA crossed through the other SMAs, we would have had several sell signals in the following month. However, this would also depend on how many months out the expiration date was on our option. If the expiration date was the next month in November (because we always sell thirty days before expiration), the signal would have suggested selling on October 10, when the price closed below the 7-day SMA.

However, the more reliable signal was not until October 20, when the 7-day SMA crossed the 20-day SMA. Yet, knowing that as we held a November option, that was slowly losing its time value (again, like that milk carton in the store's refrigerator case coming close to it sell date), we might have heeded those first stalling sell signals of the candles' dropping below the 7-day, thus retaining the largest percentage of profit.

If we had purchased a December option, we may have decided to hold through this period of consolidation, but for sure we would heed a full break of the 20-day support line if it should happen and sell, collecting the profits made from the price rising from $34.50 to $39.

If we had purchased a January or February option, we might have made the choice to hang on even longer, knowing that we had time on our side, as long as (we hope) the 50-day SMA held. As this particular scenario worked out, we would have continued to profit as the stock price rose back above $39.

We spent so much time examining this chart in order to show that no hard and fast rules exist. The choices of when to buy and sell are up to you, but you must work with the tools and information at hand.

Okay, for fun, let's throw in one more decision-making spice into the mix. If you had a December option and were planning to take a vacation on November 25, sell the option, take your profit, relax, and never give another thought to what is happening to the market while you are away. That's the beauty of trading options. You are free to move in and out of the option market, based on what is most important to you at the time. Remember, this is all about quality of life, so you sell and take your profit and have a great time while you're away.

In addition to SMAs, there are also EMAs, Exponential Moving Averages. Some traders prefer one over the other, but in theory they work the same way; they create a picture of price movement and act as lines of support and resistance.

Understanding Option Chains

To broaden our understanding of option expiration months, let's take a second look at an option chain, building on our earlier understanding. Time has value, and if we purchase an option farther away from the present date, we can expect to pay more for the benefit of that time (giving time for our stock to move in its trending direction).

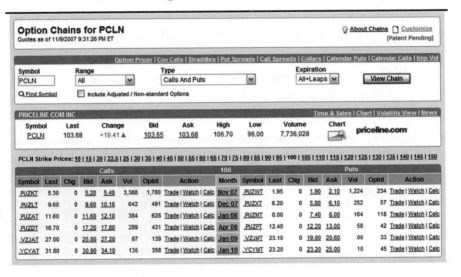

Graph courtesy of optionsXpress.com

This chain is a comparison chain for Priceline (PCLN). The current month November option for the strike price of $100 costs $5.40 (ask price), or a total cost of $540 for a contract of 100 shares.

It is expressed as: .PUZKT = PCLN NOV 100 Call

If we were to decide that we would rather purchase a December option at the same strike price of $100, the cost for that option (.PUZLT) would be $10.10 (ask price), instead of $5.40. That's an additional $4.70 for the extra month, for a total cost of $1,010, $470 more than the November option.

From the graph above, we can see that a January option would cost $12.10, a total of $1,210. An April option would be $17.80. The difference between the current month premium and the premium for April is $12.40 (that is the difference between $5.40 and $17.80) or $1,240 in total for the option contract.

So, we ask the ultimate question—Is it worth $1,240 to have an additional six months for the stock to move farther above $100, generating a profitable option?

Priceline's current stock price in this example is $103.68. It is already $3.68 in-the-money at the $100 strike price. So the choices we are presented with, after studying Priceline's chart, is how long do we want to hold the option, giving it the opportunity to rise in price, based on its past performance?

After looking at the chart, we might be able to see it often rises for two months before dropping to catch its breath. If we want to hold it until April, we must also ask whether that option of time is worth the additional total cost of $1,240. This additional time is like insurance, giving the stock time to weather minor downward adjustments in price as it advances.

Remember, though, just because this option goes out to April, that doesn't mean that we must hold it until then. We can sell at any point along the line that we think is to our benefit. In other words, we could reap a profit before a change in the stock's direction or we would sell to limit a loss.

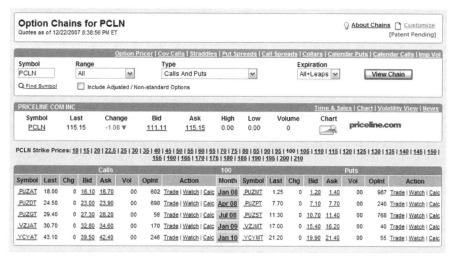

Graph courtesy of optionsXpress.com

We are still four months away from our April expiration date, but let's see how our option is doing. .PUZDT cost us $17.80 in November when we bought it. As of December 22, as seen on the option chain above, our option is now worth $23.90 a share or an increase of $6.10 per share ($610 for the 100 shares.) In the month and a half that we've held our option, it has earned a profit of 34% above our original investment.

We can chose to sell if Priceline's chart indicates that a change is imminent, collecting our profit, or we can hold longer if the chart indicates that the stock will continue to rise.

Long and Short Moving Average Crossovers

You no doubt have noticed that chart price swings create peaks and valleys. These price variations and major shifts in trend direction bring about long and short moving average crossovers. *Crossovers* are a prime indicator of trading opportunities. As mentioned earlier, trades are made in the direction of the shortest moving average crossover as it pierces the longer moving average.

When a *long trading signal* is recognized, we can consider purchasing a new long (call) position. Arrows pointing upward are long signals and we would purchase calls, expecting the price of the underlying to go up in value.

When *short signals* are generated, we would open a new short (put) position. Arrows pointing downward are short signals and we would purchase puts, expecting the price of the underlying to go down in value.

Depending on the underlying instrument, crossovers can be a reliable signal. This works well with a chart that clearly shows a trend or that swings up and down in price over the course of a month or more. What we are watching here is the 7-day SMA crossing up or down over the other SMAs. Notice on the chart below how the 7-day SMA crosses up through the other SMAs in mid-July giving us a buy signal, and then crosses down in mid-December, giving a sell signal or a signal to purchase a put.

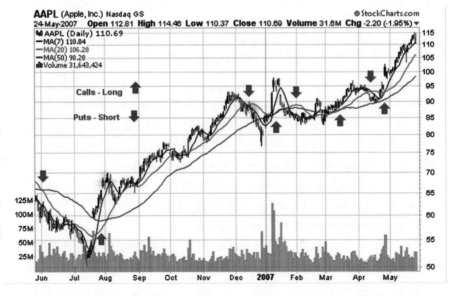

Chart courtesy of StockCharts.com

As a reliable indicator, MA (moving average) crossovers work less well in a flat or channeling market. If a stock or index is oscillating in price, but essentially trading within a channel, the crossing moving averages may cause us to be whipsawed in and out of trades. For this reason, the moving average template is not universally effective, just as no one technical indicator is effective in all market conditions. The chart below shows an area from February to April where the MAs were too close to move in and out effectively.

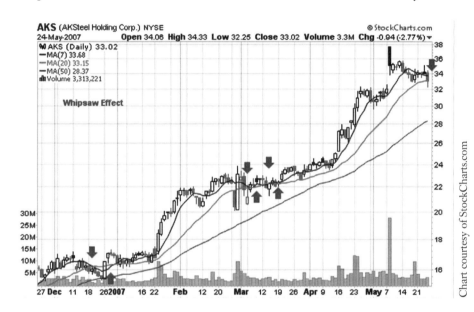

We see the effect of whipsaw when the short and long signals appear so rapidly that the trade positions haven't had time to develop and appreciate in value before the direction changed, giving the signal to close the position. Moving average crossovers combined with other determinants confirm when trades should be opened.

Confirmation refers to the use of additional indicators which must be in agreement with or confirm the primary indicator before opening a trade. We recommend choosing about three templates or a series of indicators combined on a chart to use during different trading climates. The crossover technique works very well a large percentage of the time; looking back at past swings in movement will determine if this is a reliable choice in a particular trading situation.

So, next we move on to a few of the confirming indicators to use along with the moving average crossover.

Chapter Five

INDICATORS AND OSCILLATORS

It's time to pause and take a deep breath. You may be absorbing all this like a sponge, but it's also likely that some details are swirling down the drain. You're taking in a great deal of information, and it will take time to understand it, and then more time to apply it. So, don't worry about remembering it all now. Once you analyze the charts as the book continues, information will beginning fitting into place. If you want greater understanding of the details, you can go back and review the chapters.

We've found that after reading charts for even a short period of time, the content and indicators will form patterns that your eye and mind will recognize, assimilate, and filter through. You will soon form an immediate impression about the underlying instrument and determine if it's a ripe trading candidate, in which case, it needs further consideration. This is what helps you move on or, as important, stop to take a closer look. So, trust us, shortly you'll be an expert who knows exactly what these indicators are telling you.

Relative Strength Index (RSI)

Earlier, we spoke of relative strength in reference to the IBD and a company's relative strength (RS) within its industry. A Relative Strength Index (RSI) as a momentum oscillator, compares the magnitude of a stock's recent gains to the magnitude of its recent losses and turns that information into a number that ranges from zero to one hundred.

An RSI chart has been added to the chart below. As a crossover of the moving averages takes place, look for the RSI movement to be heading in the same direction as the crossover before entering a trade. If the 7-day

MA is crossing up, cutting through the 20-day, then the RSI indicator line should be in agreement with an up turned direction. If a vertical line is drawn at the point of the cross and potential trade entry point, the RSI should be in harmony as far as direction. If it is not, it often indicates that the signal is false or weak and the movement will quickly be reversed.

Note: Within the RSI equation, the gains and losses are not divided by the total gains/losses giving a true average, but are divided by a specified number of time periods, and often this number is fourteen.

There are three ways to analysis the information on the RSI graph. Using seventy and thirty as overbought and oversold levels respectively, we are able to determine where the stock resides at the moment. (We provide additional information on overbought and oversold conditions later.)

0–30 = Oversold

100–70 = Overbought

• If the RSI rises above thirty, it is considered *bullish* for the underlying stock or index, showing that the stock is being bought, thus bringing it out of an oversold condition.

• Conversely, if the RSI falls below seventy, it is a *bearish* signal, showing that the stock is being sold, which will decrease its price value, bringing it out of its overbought condition.

If the long term trend is bullish, then an oversold reading (rising up past thirty) could mark a potential call entry point. A reading that drops below seventy is bearish and could mark a potential option exit point or an opportunity to purchase a put.

The RSI graph can also generate buy and sell signals by looking for positive (agreement) and negative divergences (disagreement) between the RSI and the underlying stock or index as seen in the candlesticks. For example, consider a rising stock whose RSI drops from a high point of eighty-five down to, say, seventy-five. Because of how the RSI is constructed, the underlying stock or index might still be rising but will often reverse its trend direction soon after such a divergence.

Bullish or bearish divergence means a discrepancy–a moving apart. In technical analysis, the terms describe the discrepancy between the trends in an indicator and the actual underlying's price.

• Bullish divergence occurs when the indicator is moving higher while the price is moving lower.

• Bearish divergence is when the indicator is moving lower while the price is moving higher.

This principle can be applied to many indictors, one of which is RSI; we'll describe others later.

In addition to the divergence (disagreement) with an underlying stock or index' price, we can also extend a line over the tops and under the bottom of the RSI reading to determine overall RSI trend.

• *Negative divergence* reflects ever-decreasing highs (lower-highs, the mounds keep getting smaller) and this usually corresponds to downward price movement, actual or expected. Often this downward slanting indicator forewarns what we can expect in the near future.

• *Positive divergence* shown by a line drawn under points in an RSI reading reflects ever-decreasing lows (higher-lows, the mounds keep rising away from the bottom). This usually corresponds to upward price movement, actual or expected, in the near future.

The RSI centerline crossover, at fifty, tells us that readings above can indicate a bullish tilt and below fifty, a bearish tilt. Traders can look for a move above fifty to confirm other bullish signals or a move below fifty to confirm other bearish signals. Often the line crossing over the fifty, in one direction or the other, accompanies a big price move. Notice the candles when the line fully breaks through the fifty centerline (December 17, January 16, February 26, and March 19). Also note that the cross over the fifty centerline corresponds with a cross of the 7-day SMA over the 20-day SMA in the same direction.

Understanding Volume

In the course of reading, you've seen that we've mentioned volume. Most often, volume refers to the number of shares traded on a given day. Typically, volume is represented at the bottom of the candlestick chart, using vertical bars, one for each day or period plotted. The higher the individual bar, the more volume trading that took place.

Volume is a combination of buying and selling of shares or contracts. The strength behind a movement change in price can be ascertained by considering the number of shares transacted during the price change. For example, the average volume of a certain stock is three hundred thousand shares per day. If the share price moved up $1.50 on volume of two hundred thousand, that movement would imply weakness as compared with a $1.50 on volume of four hundred thousand. Volume fluctuates and is often higher either early or late in the life of a price trend.

Increased volume at the end of one trend rolls into the beginning of a new trend phase. On the chart above, you will see prices forming a base while volume is rising—referring to the V-shaped pattern. This is a typical scenario and signifies the beginning of the end of a down phase, leading eventually into a new uptrend. Often, this base forming creates distinguishable patterns, providing clues as to what to expect. At the end of the book, drawings will depict and describe these recognizable patterns.

In addition, to begin putting together the information that the indicators provide, note what was happen in RSI. You see negative divergence from January until April (ever-lower high bumps), signifying that the stock was losing energy and would eventually drop. On April 9, the top of the high bump on the RSI was much lower than it had been previously (below the seventy line), pinpointing that the end was near. Note, too, the big price jumps as the RSI line crossed the fifty, heading down on April 25 and back up on May 7.

Note: The NYSE and NASDAQ measure volume differently. For every buyer, there is a seller, so one hundred shares bought equals one hundred shares sold. The NYSE counts this as one trade and as one hundred shares. The NASDAQ counts each side, so it's two hundred shares.

Understanding Gaps

A powerful bullish indicator appears when, for the entire period, a stock both opens and closes above the previous period's high. The reverse of that situation is bearish, that is, a down gap forms as a stock both opens and closes below the previous period. This action creates what appears as a *gap*, a blank spot on the candlestick chart. These are especially significant when accompanied by high volume.

Chart courtesy of StockCharts.com

Notice the spikes in buying or selling volume that accompanied the gaps in AAPL's chart above.

On the chart below, the upside gap on March 30 came with news that the FDA voted in favor of DNDN's (Denderon) new cancer drug. Then, the fall on May 8 came about because of the FDA's request for more data before its scheduled May 15 approval date.

Chart courtesy of StockCharts.com

Like the DNDN example, we often see both upside and downside gaps form when significant news is released about the company being charted. When a great deal of either buying or selling enthusiasm has built up between the closing of one daily session and the opening of the next, a continuation gap may form. On DNDN's chart, we see two of these continuation gaps marked. They often note renewal of an ongoing trend.

Another scenario indicated by a gap can signal a point at which to exit a trade. For example, if you have been in a long trade (call) that has gone well for an unusually extended period of time, the appearance of a gap would signal that things were heating up and

Wise Option Traders Remember

When trading in a mature trend, a gap in the direction of the trend often alerts us to the eminent end of that trend—it's the good-bye song.

it's time to leave the kitchen. This is why–at the point when a trend becomes exhausted, we often see a flurry of buying in an uptrend or selling on a downtrend. It's the flaming candle on the cake that's about to be eaten.

Understanding Oscillators

Oscillators are a group of chart indicators that primarily swing from one extreme of their scale to the opposite in exaggerated response to movement in price. An oscillator's course is usually drawn in a separate window on the chart, so its movement can be seen in relation to the candlesticks. As the stock price moves up and down, the oscillator line will also move, but in a magnified manner, causing it to swing from one extreme to other. Oscillators form a visible picture that is easily read.

Overbought and Oversold

Stock prices often move in cyclical patterns over time. Much of this movement is caused by market sentiment or the psychological aspects of greed and fear that we discussed earlier, particularly in the short term.

An oscillator determines when a market is in an overbought or oversold condition. When the oscillator line reaches an upper extreme, the stock or index is overbought. When the oscillator line reaches a lower extreme, the market is oversold.

> **Wise Option Traders Remember**
> *Greed and panic reign supreme, but Wise Option Traders cool our emotions and make decisions based on our charts.*

In the last chapter, we discussed support and resistance (floors and ceilings), and by using oscillators, we are able to spot the areas of support and resistance from a different angle.

Overbought is a technical condition that occurs when prices are considered too high, not sustainable, and apt to decline. A sharp price advance from, say, $20 to $35 in two weeks might lead to an overbought condition. So, when you study your chart and see that the RSI exceeds seventy, a stock might be considered to be overbought. It is important to keep in mind that overbought does not necessarily mean bearish, but merely implies that a stock has risen too far too fast and might be due for a pullback (the need to catch its breath before further advances.)

Oversold also is a technical condition and is the reverse of being over-bought. An oversold condition occurs when prices are considered too low and ripe for a rally. A sharp price decline from, say, from $35 to $20 in two weeks time might lead to an oversold condition. When the RSI drops below thirty, a stock might be considered to be oversold. It is also impor-tant to keep in mind that oversold does not necessarily mean bullish, but merely implies that the stock fell too far too fast and may be due for a reaction rally.

The terms overbought and oversold could be rephrased as *too much buying* or *too much selling*. Because of the interplay between profit taking and new buying in relation to stock price movement, a tendency exists for stock prices to reside within a short pendulum swing, even within a longer up or downtrend. Stocks can go up one day and down the next (but perhaps less than the gain the previous day), back and forth they go, yet in the end, this two-step dance they're in adds to a main up or down trend. That means that no matter how much they zig back toward the middle and zag back again, they are still moving upward or downward. This tendency for a stock or index to return to middle ground is always present and can be used to our advantage.

Williams %R

In addition to the signs and signals given by the RSI, the *Williams %R* provides a visual barometer of oversold/overbought conditions. The full scale of Williams %R oscillator is from 0 to –100.

- Zero signifies full overbought and –100 signifies full oversold.

- The –50 level is the balance point or neutral ground.

- Extremely overbought runs from –20 to zero. Extremely oversold is –80 to –100.

The following charts show extreme overbought and oversold conditions on the Williams %R. We also display the RSI graph, putting it over the main chart, so that we can compare the two to see how they can work together to predict in what direction the stock price might flow.

Utilizing the Williams %R, trading signals are generated as the Williams % R line traces up through the overbought reference line of –20 or drops below the oversold reference line of –80. Once the line reaches the oversold section we watch for the sign that it is ready to move out of that area as stock buyer's purchase the stock, sending it back up in price. When it reaches the overbought area, we watch for the sign that it is ready to drop down from that area as stock owners sell their stock, causing the stock to drop in price.

Look at the chart below and see if you can spot the signals to purchase calls (expecting prices to go up.) Also, find the signals to sell those calls before the price drops to adjust from its position as overbought.

Chart courtesy of StockCharts.com

At the arrows on the chart on page 67, Williams %R gave false buy signals. The line moved up out of the oversold area on the chart, but note that the RSI did not confirm the buy signal. It showed negative divergence for that period, nullifying the buy signal. RSI and Williams %R should agree in their direction. The signals were confirmed several days later when the RSI changed direction to agree with the movement direction of the Williams %R.

Some traders use a Williams %R crossover at the fifty line as a trigger to purchase calls or sell them when it crosses downward, but a day or two of trading is often lost by this point in the momentum either up or down.

Here are additional charts to help you begin to see the correlation between indicators:

Moving Average Convergence and Divergence (MACD)

The *MACD* is another indicator that either confirms or contradicts the signals given by the moving averages. As a momentum indicator, it's one of the simplest and most reliable indicators available.

The MACD is a *lagging indicator,* meaning it uses information based on a stock's past performance. This lagging indicator turns into a momentum oscillator and functions by tracking the amount of difference between the short-term moving averages and a longer-term moving average, often the 12-day MA and the 26-day MA. The results form a line that oscillates above and below zero, without any upper or lower limits.

This equation is represented by a thick line. The other time period is included as a reference point, seen as a thinner line. If the MACD is positive and rising, then the gap between the referenced time periods widens.

- When the thicker line moves up, positive (bullish) momentum is building for that underlying stock or index.

- When the thicker line moves downward, then the negative gap is widening, so we see negative price (bearish) momentum.

- When the thicker line crosses upward over the thinner line, we see that as a signal to buy. This buy signal will often confirm other buy signals depicted on the chart.

- But, when the thicker line crosses the thinner line in a downward slope, we see a signal to sell, depending on the option's expiration time frame.

You'll see two graphs within the MACD chart. One is formed by moving averages and the other is a *histogram,* which notes what has transpired previously on a shorter trigger exponential moving average (EMA).

The *histogram* is the bar chart along the bottom of the MACD graph. The size of the bars fluctuate above and below the zero line. These bars are another way of expressing the relationship between the MACD equation and an equation using a 9-day exponential moving average.

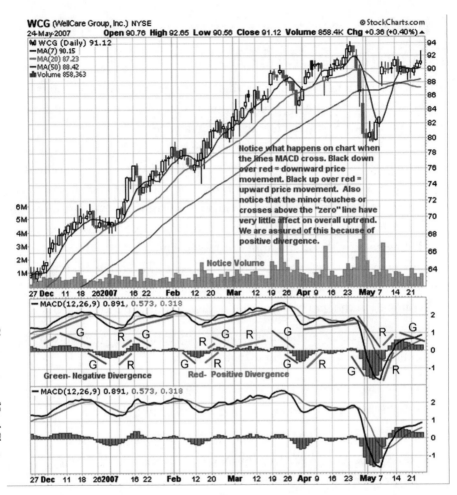

We have repeated the MACD, so we could mark one and leave the other clear to see the crossovers. Notice the crossovers of the thicker line over the thinner MACD line and how it is reflected in histogram. If the value of the MACD is greater than the 9-day EMA, the histogram will be above zero, or positive. If the value of the MACD is less than the 9-day EMA, the histogram will be below zero, or negative. These bars measure the divergence between the MACD's equation and the insertion of histogram's 9-day EMA.

You will note on the chart that the MACD histogram's movements are relatively independent of the actual MACD lines. Sometimes the MACD is falling while its histogram is rising. The histogram does not reflect the absolute value of the MACD, but rather the value of MACD relative to the 9-day EMA. Usually, because of the short time frame, but not always, a move on the MACD is preceded by a corresponding move in its histogram.

Earlier, we discussed positive and negative divergence; those same sloping lines can be noted or drawn on both the MACD and its histogram.

There are five signals in the histogram to watch for.

1. Positive divergence that precedes a bullish moving average crossover on the MACD. A positive divergence (ever higher lows) in the histogram indicates that the MACD is strengthening and could be on the verge of a crossover.

2. Negative divergence (ever lower highs) that precedes a bearish moving average crossover. A negative divergence in the histogram indicates that the MACD is weakening in momentum.

3. Broadly speaking, a widening gap indicates strengthening momentum and a shrinking gap indicates weakening momentum. Usually, a change in the histogram precedes any change in the MACD.

4. The main signal generated is a divergence on the histogram followed by a moving average crossover.

5. Keep in mind that a centerline crossover on the histogram represents a moving average crossover for the MACD.

The size of the histogram bars and the shape they create give visual clues, representing the expected movement of the moving averages. In the following chart, note the slant divergence (up or down) and peak and trough divergence.

The drawbacks or downside to MACD's histogram is that it is a second derivative, based on the MACD's equation of the price action of the underlying stock or index. The further removed an indicator is from the underlying price action, the greater chance of a false signal.

Because the histogram was designed to anticipate MACD's signals, the temptation exists to jump the ring of the timer. But, by acting only on daily signals that are in agreement with weekly signals, we are assured of trading with the longer trend and not against it. Histogram signals need to be taken as part of a whole evaluation.

Percentage Price Oscillator (PPO)

We present this oscillator to give you a choice later on about which oscillator you prefer, MACD or PPO. The *PPO* is similar to the MACD but uses a more complex, but more reliable formula; it's based on the percentage difference between two moving averages over a given period of time. It, too, uses two lines, one thicker and one thinner, to display its information. On occasion, one charting source or another will reference the PPO instead of MACD, and we want you to understand that if you can read one, you can read the other.

- If the shorter moving average (the thicker, dark line) is above the longer moving average (the thinner, lighter colored line), the PPO histogram will be above the zero line, or positive.

- If the shorter moving average is below the longer moving average, the PPO histogram will be below the zero line, or negative. The

PPO histogram compares the PPO number equation with the 9-day EMA.

• If the value of the PPO is greater than the 9-day EMA, the histogram will be above the zero, or positive.

• If the value is less than the 9-day EMA, the histogram will be below the zero, or negative.

Below is a chart that has both MACD and PPO graphs to compare. The differences are subtle and perhaps seen most clearly on the histograms.

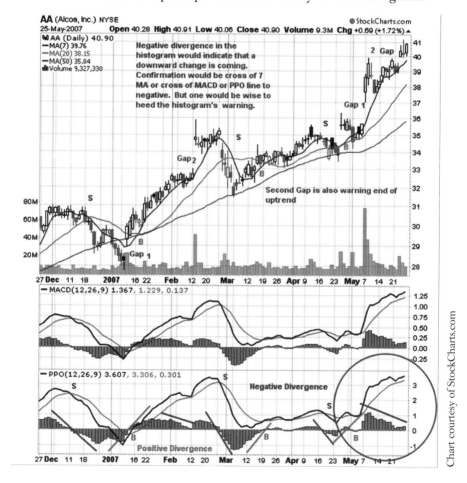

Notice that the next chart is a continuation chart (further out in time) of the Alcoa (AA) chart above. We include it to show what happened after the second gap up on the right side of the chart. Did the second warning gap precede a fall?

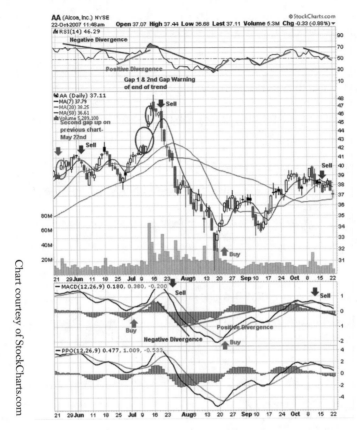

The chart above also notes buy and sell signals based on MACD or PPO crosses and areas of divergence. These signals will help you begin to recognize these patterns. The PPO is used to confirm suspected trend changes. If the thick, dark line is moving up, it is a bullish sign. If it is moving down, it is bearish.

We can note significant points on the PPO and MACD when the histogram flattens out (gets super small) and then crosses the zero line, or when the thicker line crosses the thinner line. Depending whether the crosses are up or down, they are giving a buy or sell signal.

Wise Option Traders Remember
If the cross takes place at or near the zero line, the stronger the trend.

The PPO chart can also be used to compare the strength of one stock, index, or ETF to the strength of another.

Note: The APO, or *Absolute Price Oscillator,* uses a simpler formula than PPO, but is equivalent to MADC.

Understanding Stochastics

Like William's %R, *stochastics* is a measure of momentum, and is one of the best and most reliable we have. As with the Williams %R, stochastics often concentrates on fourteen days of price activity, and spreads the lows and highs over a range, enabling us to see the price momentum, relative to its own momentum over a two-week period of time (thick, dark line.)

The stochastics or STO range is the opposite of Williams %R, with zero at the bottom, and one hundred at the top.

- Anything under twenty may indicate that the price has been sold down to the lowest *oversold* range for the previous two-week period of time.

- Anything over eighty may indicate that the price has been bought up into the highest *overbought* range for that two-week period of time.

A three-day moving average line (thinner) is added for reference or to act as a crossover signal or trigger.

Again, crossovers at these critical twenty and eighty points alert us to a potential trend reversal. But we have to keep in mind how the market as a whole has been performing and should never base a trading decision solely on a low or high stochastics indicator.

The market as a whole has daily and intraday swings but usually is trending up, down, or sideways. We cannot swing in and out of trades based on intraday movement of the Dow or NASDAQ, but it's only wise to be aware of where they are in their trending cycles.

The STO indicator comes in three forms—slow, fast, and full. Typically, we use slow or full stochastics. Fast STO is subject to fluctuations that may give us false signals, whipping us in and out of trades. Slow and full STOs smooth out these whipsaws to give us a more dependable picture.

On the following page is a chart showing all three versions of the stochastics to compare the differences and reliability.

You will notice that the full and slow STOs are nearly identical, where the fast is more sensitive and has many false cross signals that would send us in and out of trades. You will also note that the crosses coming down and below the eighty line correspond with downturns in trend. So, too, crosses riding above the twenty line correspond with changes leading to uptrends.

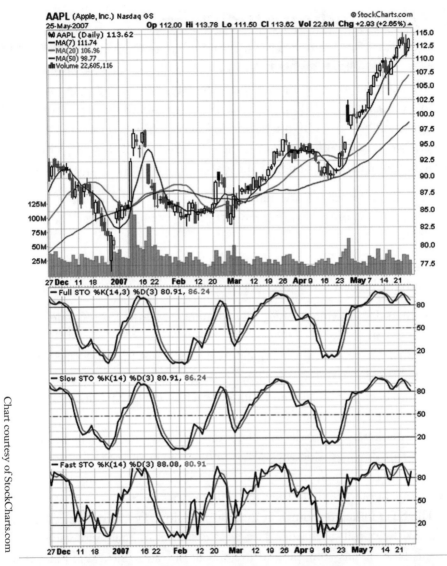

Numerous indicators and oscillators exist on which traders can choose to rely. So far, we've discussed the primary ones. We'll discuss two more briefly and add them to the mix. Each gives a different perspective on the underlying's information. Then, we'll line up the indicators and interpret the story they tell.

Average Directional Index (ADX)

The *Average Directional Index* (ADX) determines the strength of a trend, whether it's trending up or down or trading sideways. As an oscillator, the

ADX fluctuates between zero and one hundred, but readings above sixty are relatively rare. Low readings, below twenty, indicate a weak trend and high readings, above forty, indicate a strong trend.

The ADX indicator does not rate the trend as bullish or bearish, but merely assesses the strength of the current trend. In other words, a reading of forty can indicate a strong down trend as well as a strong up trend.

To determine in which direction the trend is flowing or to indicate a change in direction, two other lines are added to the graph. Usually two different colors, green for bullish and red for bearish, they represent respectively a Positive Directional Index (+DI) or Negative Directional Index (–DI). As these lines cross each other and the ADX trend line, we are able to determine not only the strength of the trend, but in which direction it will head before it fully takes place.

• When the +DI crosses upward over the –DI or the ADX trend strength line, we can expect the trend will be up.

• When the +DI line, crosses downward and the –DI moves upward and crosses over the ADX trend strength line, we can expect the trend to fall.

Chart courtesy of StockCharts.com

On the previous chart, note that although the green line marked #1 dropped lower, it never crossed the ADX line. The ADX line continued its upward direction, showing strength. The +DI line dropped, yet the bulls remained in control and after a period of adjustment, the price, reflected by the candlesticks, rose back to reach new highs.

The #2 marked on the chart shows a period of time in which, although the ADX trend strength line was still strong, the trend changed directions and the bears took control. After a big sell off, the trend lost strength and the bulls started volume buying, driving the price up again. We see this reflected by the +DI line moving back up crossing over the –DI line and the ADX line on May 12.

There is a particular reason that this ADX oscillator will be added to our chart configuration in conjunction with the MACD or PPO. When combined with the MADC or PPO a pattern is sometimes created that signals special trading opportunities.

Placing the MADC graph on top of the ADX sometimes creates an interesting pattern after a stock has gone through a strong period of selling. In actuality, however, one chart has nothing to do with the other. But we've observed the pattern, and we could call it cause and effect. It's an interesting anomaly.

Notice the thick, dark lines in both the MADC and the ADX as they come together in the charts. We have named this pattern a *squeeze,* and it's a pressure cooker of buyers and sellers; many more times than not, the squeezing pressure erupts into a new bullish period of buying or starts a new uptrend.

In the first squeeze in December, the strong pressure and momentum lasted three months. In this instance, you'll note that as the buying and selling pressure built, forcing the ADX line down and away, the ADX line quickly turned back up and rose, reflecting a new strong trend. As the ADX line rose above 20, the +DI (positive) line crossed to move above the ADX line and the –DI (negative) line dropped below the ADX line.

Let's look at the second squeeze pattern in late March. Pressure built, though not quite as tightly as in December, but nonetheless, we could figure an upward change was going to be the result. With this squeeze, the price rose from $29 to $32, which was enough of a rise to make money on an option, but in comparison the rise was short-lived. You'll notice that a full two months later the ADX line had yet to turn and rise to show strength in the new trend, and the MADC line never made it over zero. The ADX line dropped lower and the +DI and the –DI lines zigzagged, changing direction a half-dozen times as the price candlesticks moved in a horizontal trading pattern, and then, eventually, it went into another minor down trend.

Squeezes on weekly and daily charts are fairly reliable patterns that prove profitable. Once in a while–fortunately, seldom–they fizzle out. Once the lines start to spread apart, no perfect indicator of the power behind the thrust exists, but it usually moves upward. It is also interesting to note, that if a squeeze does fizzle, we often see the squeeze reform, but show much more strength the second time.

Accumulation/Distribution Line

The accumulation/distribution line is the last indicator we'll cover in this book. However, many indicators measure volume and the flow of money into or out of a particular stock or index, and accumulation/distribution is one of the most popular volume indicators.

We mentioned this accumulation/distribution in the context of the IBD, because, back when we started explaining option trading, we discussed the fact that we want option candidates that the larger institutions (the pack) support with their ongoing interest and share purchases. In other words, we're learning by using the same tools used by the large investors and we follow the trends they push into existence with their trades.

The accumulation/distribution equation ignores the change in closing price from one period to the next, but gives value to the volume as either positive or negative, focusing on the price action for each given period (day, week, or month). It is a formula that calculates value based on the location of the closing price, relative to the range for the period. Using these assigned values, an accumulation/distribution line is drawn.

Chart courtesy of StockCharts.com

The appearance of this line doesn't tell us who purchased shares, but we can use it to confirm the strength or sustainability behind an advance or to confirm weakness. As a volume indicator, the accumulation/ distribution line will help determine if the volume in a security is increasing on the advances or declining; this gives us information about how much the institutional thrust is behind the volume. So, the accumulation/distribution line can be used to gauge the general flow of money. An uptrend indicates that buying pressure is prevailing, and a downtrend indicates that selling pressure is prevailing.

As with other oscillators, lines of positive and negative divergence may be drawn to spot differences in direction from the price candlesticks, often foreshadowing change.

Now that we have come to the end of this chapter on indicators and oscillators, I want to review and draw your attention back to something we highlighted earlier with regard to the candlesticks. You no doubt have come to understand how much information can be derived from the candlesticks as to high, low, opening and closing prices, but I want to again point out the candlesticks pictures below with the long tails or shadows.

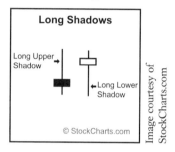

With their image in mind, skim over the last few charts above. See if you can spot candles similar in appearance and note what often happens after a day resulting in a candle with a long upper or lower tail or shadow. A candlestick like this often reflects a change in direction, or the continuation of direction, *perhaps* as soon as the next day on a daily chart or the next time period on other time-frame charts.

As explained earlier, the reason for these changes is what caused the tail or shadow in the first place. To use this as a reference above, a daily candlestick with a long shadow at the bottom shows strong buying pressure. If the candle is red (a selling day) the tail at the bottom means there was a lot of buying pressure at the end of the day, perhaps not enough to win the day, but perhaps enough to push it up the next morning. If it was a hollow candle (a buying day) with a long shadow at the bottom it, it means that although there was strong selling pressure during the day, at the end of the day, buying pressure was strong enough to win the day and will likely to continue the next day.

In reverse, if the candle is red (a selling day) with a long upper shadow, it

means though there was buying pressure, those who sold applied the stron-
gest pressure during the course of the day and are likely to do so again the
next day. If the candle is hollow (a buying day) with a long upper shadow,
it means that although buyers won the day, sellers applied a great deal
of pressure at the end of the day and are likely to do so again tomorrow,
causing the day to reverse to a down day.

Like all the other indicators we have discussed, there are no 100% guar-
antees about what we can expect from their information. They are *guideposts*,
reflecting what's happened in the past. They are markers on the measuring
cup or telltale signs that when considered with other information will help
us decide whether it is time to buy or sell.

Chapter Six

THE MATTER OF PUTS

Thus far, every time we've mentioned *puts* it's been to say that we'd talk about the subject in another chapter. Well, we've reached the right place to interject information about a subject that is often hard for new traders to grasp, let alone put to use. We sometimes refer to them as the "pesky puts," not because they don't have a legitimate place in trading (indeed they do!), but because the concept goes contrary to what you've spent a lifetime learning. Specifically, how many of us were taught that paying for something that may go down in value could be a very wise investment?

Put options are contracts that give the owner the right, but not the obligation, to sell a specified number of shares of a stock at a specified price (strike price) on or before a specified date (expiration date). Put options are purchased when the price of the underlying stock is expected to go down. This is also considered a short position because it benefits from a decline in the security's price.

Why would we consider purchasing something we expect to decrease in value? Let's use an example to explain the concept in simple terms.

Example

You and your neighbor, Bob, are in your front yard discussing the new shopping center under construction about a half mile away. You both agree that the new center will be convenient and will add value to your already appreciating property. While you're talking, a real estate agent walks up to you. She explains that she's selling pieces of paper that guarantee that if you decide to sell your home anytime over the next year she will pay $100,000 for the house, no more, no less, but the $100,000 is guaranteed. This guarantee will cost $1,000.

Bob isn't impressed. "Why the heck would I consider paying $1,000 to let you buy my property for $100,000. It's worth $99,500 now and it's been appreciating 10% every year for several years. With the new shopping center coming in, who knows? By the time that contract runs out, my house will be worth $110,000 or more."

On the other hand, you take a minute to mull over the agent's offer, which she has explained is a transferable contract, meaning that you can transfer it–give it away or sell it–to another person. As it happens, you've been thinking about moving, but haven't found a new house yet. You know your house might go up in value before you actually want to sell, but this guarantee feels like insurance. You tell the agent to get the paperwork ready while you get your checkbook. So, you pay the real estate agent $1,000 for the paper guarantee.

Two months later, you find the perfect house across town, and quickly find a buyer willing to pay $102,000 for your old house. Of course, you now feel a little foolish for purchasing the contract to sell at the lower fixed price. And Bob won't let you forget it. Nevertheless, you hang on to the contract.

Six months later, an article in your local paper reports that many years ago, toxic waste material was buried beneath the ground in your old neighborhood. This news has an immediate effect on the housing market in your town. Within days, you learn that the house you recently sold is now worth only $50,000. At that point, you remember the paper that you hold, guaranteeing a price of $100,000.

You consider going to your neighbor Bob, but his mean attitude bothers you. Instead, you go to the young family who purchased your home. "I'm sorry that this happened," you say, "but there was no way of knowing about the toxic waste. But, I have this paper and I'm willing to sell it to you for $2,000. The paper says that a particular real estate agent is obligated to purchase the house for $100,000."

Naturally, the young family is ecstatic. They will be out from under the poor investment at a loss of only $4,000–the extra $2,000 they paid you for the house, plus the $2,000 for the paper guarantee. You're happy to have sold the house and the paper.

In the eight months since you purchased that contract, you doubled the $1,000 you paid for it, so you have 100% profit.

In our example, we point out that no one could have anticipated the toxic waste situation, but that would not be entirely true with a put purchase. We purchase puts with the same care and consideration that we put into our call choices. We are drawn to a security by its chart and then we do our homework. We know its past earnings history, its next earnings report date, what sector it's included in and whether that sector is in favor at the moment or cycling out. In addition, we look up current news articles and analysts' opinions and know whether it has been recently downgraded. Guided by the security's chart, we can see that it often telegraphs its fall from grace.

Applying the Principle behind Puts

If you own the underlying stock, puts can be purchased as insurance against a stock going down in value. In our case, we don't own the underlying stock, just as we don't own the stock in the companies upon which we purchase call options. However, during our chart reading, we see a situation developing that indicates that a stock, index, or ETF might be cycling down; or, perhaps it's confronting other bad news, such as a poor earnings report, bad publicity, losing a contract, or the FDA refusing approval for a product. We can purchase a put, knowing that when the stock goes down our contract to sell shares at that higher fixed price will go up in value. The further the shares drop, the more valuable our contract becomes. Then, when our chart reading indicates that the underlying has hit a bottom, we sell our put contract before expiration and before the shares start to regain their value. When we sell our put to close our option, the stock exchanges have buyers anxious to snap it up, so they can sell their stock at its former higher price, rather than wait the time necessary for it to eventually regain its value.

When reading charts, opportunities to purchase puts are the opposite of calls. These opportunities arise when a stock is at a high point and our indicators show that the trend is about to reverse, that is, head downward. We identify many of these occasions when the MACD, PPO, ADX cross downward, becoming negative, or when the Williams %R or RSI are dropping out from being overbought.

These same indicators can point out the time to sell a call that you own. So, just as indicators can suggest the opportunity to purchase a call, they can also indicate that it is time to sell a put that you own.

In real life terms, many traders who have purchased calls on an uptrending stock, which has climbed upward over a period of months, will then purchase puts on the very same stock, riding it through the downtrend. As we've said, stocks cycle up and down. Over the course of a year some stocks may gain 20%–30% in value, yet they moved up and down, retracing that 20%–30% many times. Alert option buyers can take advantage of those swings in trend.

The Big and Small Pictures Count

If the downtrend is associated with an overall market reversal, the trend can extend over many weeks or months. If it is associated with an individual stock or Index, the downward movement might happen over a shorter period of time. Once an underlying instrument starts to lose ground, more and more fear-of-losing-profit selling takes place. This continues until the bulls jump in, believing that the underlying is now in the bargain-basement at irresistible prices.

Wise Option Traders Remember
Fear runs twice as fast as greed.

Puts are listed on the same option chain as calls. Puts are listed on the *right* side of the strike price, while calls are listed on the *left* side of the strike price.

We'll further discuss all the elements of the options chain in detail when we get into discussing which options to choose to paper-trade, virtually trade, and eventually to invest in.

As we lay all the ingredients out and read more charts together, we'll also mark the put purchasing opportunities.

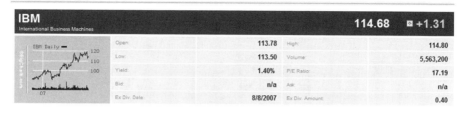

OPTION CHAIN FOR INTERNATIONAL BUSINESS MACHINES

		CALLS							PUTS				
					Hide November, 2007 Options								
Symbol	Last	Change	Vol	Bid	Ask	Open Int.	StrikePrice	Symbol	Last	Change	Vol	Bid	Ask	Open Int.
IBMKO				39.80	40.00		75.00	IBMWO					0.05	
IBMKP	35.60			34.70	35.00	24.00	80.00	IBMWP					0.05	
IBMKQ	26.60			29.80	30.10	10.00	85.00	IBMWQ	0.05				0.05	160.00
IBMKR	22.90			24.70	25.10	12.00	90.00	IBMWR	0.02	-0.07	40.00		0.10	72.00
IBMKS	17.84			19.80	20.10	96.00	95.00	IBMWS	0.15			0.05	0.10	1,047.00
IBMKT	14.60	+1.30	5.00	14.80	15.10	42.00	100.00	IBMWT	0.15	-0.10	125.00	0.15	0.20	1,931.00
IBMKA	9.80	+0.60	51.00	10.10	10.30	2,725.00	105.00	IBMWA	0.45	-0.15	206.00	0.35	0.45	2,752.00
IBMKB	5.50	+0.59	742.00	5.60	5.90	1,225.00	110.00	IBMWB	1.00	-0.54	1,369.00	1.00	1.10	7,313.00
						Stock Price ▶	114.68	Last as of 10/23/2007 4:01:00 PM						
IBMKC	2.50	+0.40	1,966.00	2.40	2.50	9,539.00	115.00	IBMWC	2.80	-0.80	525.00	2.65	2.80	15,005.00
IBMKD	0.75	+0.11	1,540.00	0.65	0.75	16,822.00	120.00	IBMWD	6.00	-1.00	92.00	5.90	6.30	7,228.00
IBMKE	0.15	-0.03	574.00	0.15	0.20	10,824.00	125.00	IBMWE	10.50	-1.40	16.00	10.40	10.60	748.00
IBMKF	0.05	-0.05	80.00	0.05	0.10	3,471.00	130.00	IBMWF	14.40			15.30	15.50	57.00
IBMKG	0.01	-0.04	1.00		0.05	1,584.00	135.00	IBMWG	19.30			20.20	20.60	10.00

Chapter Seven

PUTTING IT ALL TOGETHER—IDENTIFYING BUY SIGNALS

So, at last, we've reach the point at which we begin to delve into the mechanics of choosing the particular stocks on which to purchase options, and how to decide which type of option to buy. Based on my observations, women traveling this type of investing path for the first time confront a few issues. Throughout this book, we've offered assurances that a bit of confusion, and even feelings of trepidation are normal. This stage is no different.

Often, a woman will hit a point that she wonders how in the world she will put it all together. How will she *ever* be able to determine what the indicators are telling her? What if she identifies contradictory information? How will she sort through it all? So, we say again, hang in with us.

Here's the plan. First, we'll lay out all the indicators and oscillators. As plainly as possible we'll restate the essential details about them; then, as you see a few more charts, we will analyze the information *as if they were today's charts* and we'll work with them as if we are digesting and analyzing the information needed to make an option purchase now.

Always keep in mind that our strategy as option traders is straightforward and doesn't change. Our goal is to buy options when premium prices are low, or at least fairly priced, and to sell when prices are higher. Low or fair option premium prices doesn't necessarily equate to low or falling stock prices. Remember we buy options on solid, highly-rated companies. We also want to play it very safe so that our risk is as low as possible and our profit as high.

We also follow market trends. There was a time when most stock market players and financial experts considered the period between October and

January as bargain basement time. Today, however, any truth or accuracy in this is blurred, because financial markets are increasingly *world markets,* supported by economies outside the borders of the United States. Every day, or so it seems, the stock market expands into new global areas that were once thought to be economically underdeveloped or emerging and not yet players on a global stage.

Recently, I heard about a fifty-seven-year study that emphasized the adages mentioned above. It used the Dow Industrial Average Index (DIA). Going back to 1950, they calculated two $10,000 portfolios. Each purchased the same thirty Dow stocks, and in the early years, those would have been different stocks than one would purchase today. One or two stocks have rolled off the DIA each year and were replaced with new, better performing stocks.

Each year for fifty-seven years, Portfolio #1 bought $10,000 worth of stock on May 1, and sold on October 31. The study correlated the results for the fifty-seven years, and at the end, the return was $10,341. This is a terrible profit! The timing of those six months had been the seasonally weakest time. Portfolio #2 took $10,000 and bought the same stocks on November 1 and sold them on April 31, every year for the fifty-seven years period from 1950. Its return was $592,000. This is an amazing difference!

Traditionally, after this period of being beaten down from May to October, with many forming base patterns, the stocks then would be low-priced and ready to rally over the next six months. So, these early months in the new cycle beginning in October or November may still be bargain time; however, it may be that the market's cyclical pattern will be affected by other global elements. But, regardless of the elements that influence the trends, we will nevertheless follow the market's trend direction whether it takes us up or down its path.

What to Keep Your Eye On

We need to consider many things before getting involved in an actual trade, including an awareness of what's going on the *macro* world of the market–the big picture. Then, with that awareness, we narrow the view through a funnel in order to look at the *micro*–the small picture.

Eventually, keeping your eye on and evaluating the macro, the overall market, will become second nature. On an ongoing basis, we pose questions to see how the big picture market is doing. Where is the money flowing?

Into energy? Financial services? Technology? Healthcare? What about the indices? What's happening in the NASDAQ, the Dow Industrial Average, and the S&P 500? For the most part, these major indices represent the entire market. If the indices are down-trending–in a decline–then the individual parts of the market may be in a decline.

So, in this declining market, we'll be cautious when we're considering calls, or we may decide that it's time to purchase puts. However, every downward movement shouldn't be an automatic sign of distress in the market–and shouldn't cause you stress either. Awareness is what is called for.

Sometimes price corrections occur on these Indices, following a longer upward or downward trend. We hear financial reporters say, "We were due for a correction." Then, the buyers get back into the market over the next day or two and take advantage of the correction. These corrections may also accompany a change in sector; that is, a sector moving out of favor and another moving into its place. Sector changes occur when a particular sector is overbought and prices are high; the large institutions (the pack) take profits by selling their shares, and then they shift their focus to a sector that has been undervalued and has lower prices. This is how they start their buying process over again, and their shift begins to drive up the prices for the undervalued sector. As option traders, we want to take advantage of this ride up.

Let's take a look at a Dow Industrial Average chart to take in the big picture. This chart (pictured below) covers a period of one year. In retrospect, it's obvious that we can identify periods when it would have been advantageous to purchase calls and when we'd have been better served by buying puts. On occasion (but rarely) individual stocks have the strength to go against the trend of the overall market. However, it's seldom worth the risk involved in fighting the directional pull of the overall market–the big picture. (There's an old saying that only dead fish go with the flow. Well, that holds true for your spirit of adventure and trying new things, but not for your option purchases.)

You will also notice that we have added to the chart all the oscillators and indicators that we've discussed thus far. This allows you to see how they work together. You may find you only need three or four of these to make your option decisions, but in terms of the learning process, it doesn't hurt to see how they confirm or negate each other.

As you look over the chart, notice what the indicators show when the Dow experienced minor and then major adjustments. Note that the RSI dips on the small moves and drops like a rock on the big moves. Can you spot the positive and negative divergence? Note the move from the upper overbought areas on the Williams %R down to the lower oversold. On the PPO, notice how the lines snake back and forth on the small movements, and then have major crosses on the big pullbacks or climbs from the lowest of ranges.

Do you see the squeeze that appeared during March? What was the result? A climb from March until June. We see another lesser squeeze, slightly misshapen, in mid-August. The market went steadily up, but only for a month and a half before it dropped again. If you look closely, you can follow the line

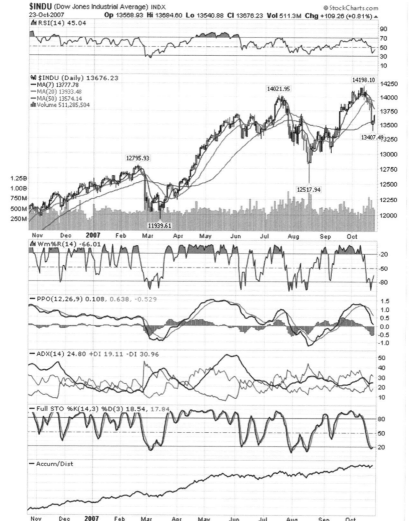

Chart courtesy of StockCharts.com

crosses on the STO. These are more easily followed on a daily, six-month chart.

The accumulation-distribution indicator shows only minor dips in its upward movement; although the INDU experienced these adjustments in March and August, the overall thrust of the market is an uptrend. These periods of sell-off, adjustments, or pullbacks, or breathers are all part of the natural life of the market as a whole and in its individual parts. We could draw trend lines from a point between February and March along the lowest lows, out to 13,500, and another parallel trend line to the 14,021.95 high peak and we would have an upward channel with a resistance level around 14,750.

The Picture Differs among the Indices

The NASDAQ includes a significant number of semiconductor industries, so a rise in the semiconductor sector can trigger a rise in the NASDAQ. On the other hand, a rise or fall in one sector in the Dow has a lesser overall affect. In addition, the oil and gas sectors, and the gold and silver markets, sometimes move inversely, or opposite from the rest of the market. So, as oil and gold rise, the Dow, the NASDAQ, the NYSE, the S&P 500, and so forth, may have a tendency to move down in price. But, we always strive to have the market on our side.

The NASDAQ composite chart below covers the same period that the Dow covered. They mirror each other in their major pullbacks because market sentiments have a tendency to spread between the indices. But, with some regularity, the Dow has a down day and the NASDAQ rises over the same period. It all depends on the sectors and individual components.

For comparison, we include a chart for the S&P for the same year period. This chart also mimics both the Dow and NASDAQ in its appearance, yet at times, its movements appear more exaggerated. On the Dow, at times the daily price can swing one hundred points or more. On the NASDAQ, the swing can be in the low- to mid-double digits. The S&P can experience high single digits to low double digit gains or losses.

Noticing and Comparing Trends

Notice that we could draw channels on the NASDAQ and S&P as well, depicting an uptrend of trading within the channels for all three indices. A breakout from these channel-lines of resistance or support, either to the up or downside, will be significant to the future direction of the market.

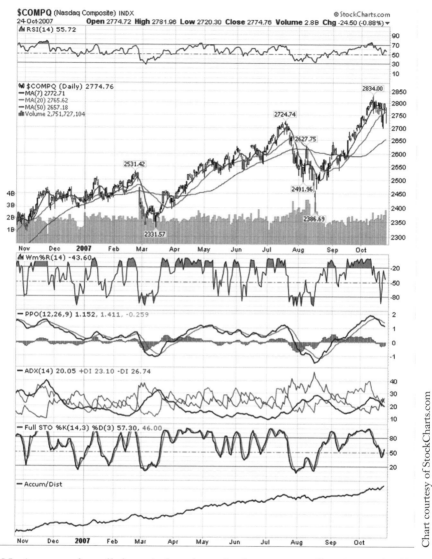

Chart courtesy of StockCharts.com

Notice, too, that all three index charts had squeezes of buying and selling pressure. As these squeezes played out, the indices started new uptrends. We point this out again, because a squeeze seen on a chart of one of your option candidates is a strong signal that the underlying will experience an indefinite period of uptrending movement.

The length of uptrend time is variable, but in the majority of cases it is a sure signal of upcoming upward movement, maybe days, weeks, or months. There are times that this squeezing pressure will become tighter before it pops, but the expected burst is as close to a guarantee as you can get in stock movement.

✳A Strategy in Action

In your search for reliable underlying candidates, locate a security that, while uptrending, has had a minor pullback in price, but preferably one that has not broken the support of the 50-day MA. Touching the 50-day MA can often be a springboard for regaining momentum and moving further upward. Wait for that pullback in price. In addition, with the pullback, look for developing squeezes.

Buy Signals–Calls

Daily Chart

Consider trading long (call) with confirmed uptrend with the 7-day MA on top, the 20-day MA in the middle, and the 50-day MA on the bottom, buying in at a pullback, confirmed by the indicators below.

- Trade long at a channel breakout (breaking through an upper resistance line), with increased volume.

- A gap up, with increased volume early in an uptrend.

- Price candlestick breaking upward through moving averages, (7-day moving up through 20-day or 50-day), with increased volume.

- Reversal of an oversold condition within a longer trend, confirmed by the following indicators.

  - The RSI line should be curved and moving up from the bottom area above 30 and toward or crossing the 50.

  - A reversing candlestick's close should be fully above the 7-day SMA.

  - Williams %R should be in the oversold range, and starting to turn, crossing the –80 line, returning back up.

  - The MACD or PPO line crosses the line, heading upward. The closer the cross is to the zero or over it, the stronger the momentum. The histogram confirms the cross when it moves over the zero line.

  - The positive +DI line crosses the ADX upward. Or the green line should be above the black ADX line.

  - Stochastics should be in the bottom oversold range, and starting to turn back up over the 20 and moving into the 50 range. Sometimes there is a double spike around the 20 range before a trend change.

  - Accumulation/distribution line should be heading upward, the higher the better.

Weekly Charts

To get a broader view and further confirmation, double-check that all the positive signals you've seen in an individual underlying security's daily chart are confirmed on the weekly. The macro picture should agree with the micro. Later, in the chapter about chart patterns, we will list buy points that appear on the weekly charts.

Buy Signals–Puts

Consider purchasing short (put) with confirmed downtrend with 7-day SMA on the bottom, 20-day SMA in the middle, and 50-day SMA on the top. Look for the following.

- Downside breakouts of channels (a drop through the support line), with increased volume.

- Gaps down, with increased volume early in a downtrend.

- Price candlestick breaking downward through moving averages (7-day down through 20-day or 50-day), with increased volume.

- Reversal of an overbought condition within a longer downtrend, confirm by the following indicators:

  □ RSI line should be in the upper area, heading down.

  □ A reversing candlestick should fully close below the 7-day MA.

  □ Williams %R is in the high overbought range, –20 or above, and starting to turn back down.

  □ MACD or PPO line heading down and crossing the other line. The histogram confirms the cross when it moves under the zero line.

  □ Stochastics should be in the higher overbought range, above the 80 line, and starting to move back down.

  □ Accumulation/distribution line should be heading down, the lower the better.

Weekly Charts

To get a broader view and further confirmation, double-check that all the positive signals you've seen in an individual underlying security's daily chart are confirmed on the weekly. The macro picture should agree with the micro. Later, in the chapter about chart patterns, we will discuss put buy points that appear on the weekly charts.

Keep Your Eye on the Charts

After we look at a few charts, checking out the history, and then evaluating them as potential option buying candidates, we'll focus on sell signals.

Since our first rule is to be aware of what the overall market is doing, the first charts we study are daily Indices' charts.

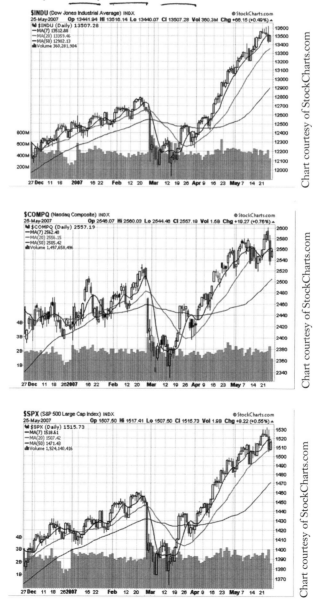

Looking at the charts, we can see that on February 27, 2007, the market made a four-hundred-point correction, and then over the next two months recovered and continued upward to gain another seven hundred points. Prior to the adjustment in February, the market had climbed steadily upward since the previous July. That is quite a long uptrend with only one correction of consequence.

Expanding our view beyond the charts above, the market has been in an overall uptrend since March of 2003, the longest uptrend in history, taking the Dow from 7,416 to over 14,000. During this period there have been numerous corrections to serve as examples, yet an eight-month-sprint without an adjustment had investors and fund managers holding their collective breath, waiting for the correction.

This brings us up to May (the present, for our purposes, given the date on the chart). On all three indices' charts we can see days of profit-taking during May. Support has held at the 20-day SMA, but after such a long uptrend, we need to question whether we might be getting to the nosebleed area of this trend.

We certainly called this accurately; nosebleed area was an understatement, considering the major market correction (40 percent) in late 2008 and 2009. These downturns are complex and hard to predict.

Volatile up-and-down market movement affects our option decisions. We should examine the trends and ask probing questions. If we purchase a call option at this time, will the underlying stock or Index have time to rise again, thereby bringing us a profit? Of course, we always have the chance to purchase a put if the market drops to change its course into a downtrend. But, if we believe the market will fall only a little bit, making a temporary correction within the ongoing uptrend, we would want to purchase a call option with an expiration date out far enough for it to have time to increase in value or give us insurance should the market go against our well laid plan.

The big question–*What will the market do?* We can't know for sure, but we look over its history, using that as a loose guide as we weigh the current situation. If it's too volatile, we can step aside for awhile until the market adjusts. We can't lose real money from the sidelines. While we might miss an opportunity, we won't lose cold, hard cash.

Again, based on volatility, if we decide the potential profit is worth the risk, then when our option makes a profit within a few days (a week) we *sell*, rather than hold trying to squeeze the last drop of juice out that lime. *Be happy with 20%–30%–40%–50% profit earned in a few days and save the desire for big profits of 100%+ for more predicable times.*

We speak from experience. More than once, we have earned a nice profit in a couple days, but with lots of time left before our option expiration date, that swayed us to hang on to make more money, and then the market turned. Our profits evaporated and never returned to that profitable level before time ran out. And, even if, on occasion, it did eventually reach that level again, selling earlier would have been the better strategy from a psychological viewpoint. Being satisfied with the earlier profits would have saved days or weeks of nail biting and teeth gnashing–and cheerleading from the sidelines–as the stock crawled back upward.

2. The Final Factors

Our final decisions should be based on the individual stock, ETF, or Index itself and how it looks relative to the market as a whole. We've listed a few charts, leaving them without annotations, so that you can evaluate their potential as an option candidates. Then, we'll discuss what we see below the chart.

Flip to Cree's chart on page 100 and then come back to read further. Let your eye roam around the chart, studying the most recent activity. Where possible, notice the indicator details and evaluate what they're telling you.

Starting at the top of the chart, the RSI is high (above 70) in the oversold area. At times, securities can reside in overbought or oversold areas for weeks, but in the case of this stock, it seems to rotate between overbought and oversold over the course of a month or so. The peak on the RSI during the period of April 23 seems to be a bit higher than the high peak on May 21. This reflects negative divergence, but on a minor scale. One would expect that since the stock made a new high on this day, the RSI would also reflect a higher high; however, that didn't happen, at least not yet, which gives reason to pause to look more closely at the other indicators.

The candlesticks tell us Cree's stock runs in the low $20 range. Certainly, we can make a profit on a $20 stock, but to a lesser degree than a more expensive stock. On the May 21, a high volume event took place, reflected by the long candle. This jump in price happened in one day after three weeks of declining prices; the jump brought us even with the high price before that decline. The previous high would have been a point of resistance, but the price would probably move higher because of the volume thrust present in that one day movement. It did move higher on May 22 and 23. Having reached another new high, there was a little profit taking on May 24, which brings us to the last candle and close to another high.

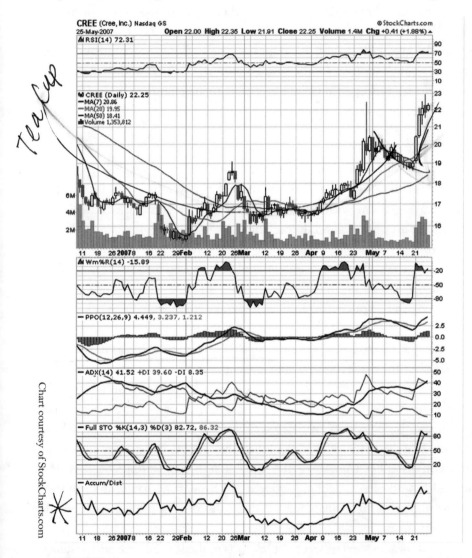

Based on the indicators below the chart, we must try to determine whether this stock will continue its uptrend or, as the RSI suggests, whether the uptrend is weakening. This stock's price movement is rather erratic, with no clear uptrend or downtrend in the last six months. The company manufactures semiconductors and its stock has fluctuated up and down. A long view of this chart would show that it dropped off a high of $34 in April of 2006, and since November of 2006, the stock has been forming a large pattern called a *cup and handle*. (Notice the broad cup-bowl shaped pattern; it's high on the left side and high on the right side, with the middle curved into the bottom of the cup.)

The highest, high point of the left of the cup was at $23, which is near the current price on this chart. So, this is a pattern that has been more than six months in the making, and we are at a point where it will soon break above that point. This would be a sign that the pattern has been completed and is now ready to move on.

As of May 21, the SMAs are lined up in the order of an uptrend.

- The Williams %R has just reached the overbought area. Based on the visible repeated pattern seen on the Williams, Cree could remain in this area for two or three weeks.

- The PPO is just at a point where it will cross to the upside and is doing so above the zero line, which gives this uptrending movement a stronger momentum.

- The ADX line is heading upward and the Green (+DI = Positive) line is ready to cross the ADX line heading up, reflecting this upward momentum.

- The Full STO has risen out of the oversold area and reached overbought territory. It could stay there for a few weeks.

- Also, the accumulation/distribution line is heading upward and rising showing there is growing buying interest in this stock.

After analyzing the information on this chart, we can see that except for the lower dollar price per share of this stock, its conditions would qualify, making this stock a good candidate for purchasing an option contract. At the same time, as a candidate, Cree requires that we watch carefully to monitor its daily conditions because it appears easily swayed by daily stock market movement. Cree is not a stand alone stock–the rebel–that stands defiant against the flow. If the market dips, Cree is apt to drop as well, so we'd advise taking profits at the first opportunity with a fall in price. In addition, since Cree is part of the oil sector, we must stay on top of what's happening with oil prices. Is the price per barrel going up or down?

In the second half of 2007, oil prices went from the mid-$50 a barrel to record-breaking prices of nearly $100 a barrel at the time of this writing. Certainly this price movement has favorably affected stock prices of all the industries included in this sector and others on the periphery, such as shipping and transport companies.

Let's see how we did with our analysis. The chart below shows the next six months of trading days. The candlesticks furthest to the right on the chart above are now the candlesticks furthest to the left on the chart below, but they reflect the same period of time.

The stock went up from May 21 to June 3, going from $22 to $27.50. For the four days after this high, the stock dropped in price; on the second down day the stock closed fully below the 7-day MA. Depending on our expiration date, it may have been advisable to sell here. We would have made a profit, but it would be down from its highest mark.

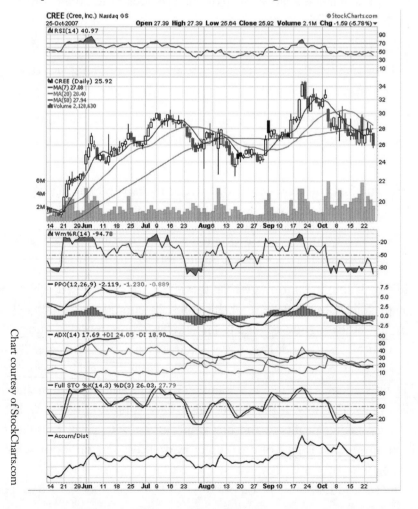

If expiration were several months out, we might have decided to hold and see how things developed. Day three it went up a few cents, days four and five it dropped another twenty-five cents or so, but then reversed to climb for the next month and a half.

It climbed up to $30 before it dropped to form a new pattern. Earlier, we mentioned a cup pattern. Can you see the slightly bumpy, yet rounded bottom of a cup between July 16 and September 17?

Another Chart to Analyze

Let's analyze another chart, this one for TSO, a petroleum refining and marketing company. (In a later chapter, we'll list Internet sites where you

Chart courtesy of StockCharts.com

can look up information about a company's activities, products, services, history, dividends, analysts' opinions, and so forth.)

The RSI on this chart shows upward movement above the 50, but below 70, or the overbought range. The RSI confirms that this stock has been in an extended uptrend, with consistent buying, keeping the RSI line in the overbought range for the last three or four months, until this last month of May.

At the $120 range, this is a higher priced stock. You'll note that the candlesticks in this stock often represent $2 to $5 movements during a single day. The candlesticks also depict the uptrend since the beginning of 2007. From the first of May, some profit taking occurred after this long stretch up. By profit taking, we mean that some of the pack sold a portion of the shares they held and garnered some profit, leaving a portion of their holdings to reap further rewards. This represents the practice of not keeping all of the eggs in one basket until it is overflowing and too heavy to hold, or we have too many shares to sell quickly. It is also interesting to note that when the Dow dropped four hundred points on February 27, this stock barely budged from its upward course.

The SMAs are lined up 7-day, 20-day, and 50-day, though it's hard to tell if the 7-day is really above or just cruising right on top of the 20-day. No matter; it's close enough not to be a firm break down through the 20-day.

Williams %R is in the mid-range, above 50. It, too, shows that this stock can remain in the overbought area for long periods of time.

After cycling down for the last two weeks the PPO is now moving up and near a cross, above the zero line.

Note: *Nearly* crossing and a *real cross* are not equivalent. It is better to wait another day until the line actually crosses over. At times, the PPO line gets so close, close enough to kiss, but doesn't cross. It will even slide along, running parallel for a time and then drop back down. Rather than jump the mark on a near cross, and then wait for it to actually happen, leaving you to wring your hands together as you wait, hoping and praying that it will eventually move back up, we urge you to practice patience, wait for the cross—it's the better choice.

In this chart, the PPO histograms are getting small and coming closer to the zero, confirming the positive upward movement. But since it hasn't crossed the zero line yet, again, it's better to watch until it makes the cross.

The ADX line is actually showing some weakness; we see negative divergence, contrary to the three last days of buying. The line tapers downward, against the other indicators that show upward movement. This could be a sign that the overall upward trend is growing fatigued, or it could be residual negativity from the pullback during the first weeks of May. The +DI line has turned and is not confirming upward trending momentum.

The Full STO has crossed upward and is at the 50 line, all confirming upward growth, However, it's taken a sideways turn, running horizontal at the moment, as if trying to make up its mind which way it will go.

The accumulation/distribution line is at a high interest area.

Based on the information of this chart, TSO is definitely a candidate worth watching, but wait for the sure signs of a cross on the PPO.

But what if we'd have purchased an options contract in January 2007, with a June or July expiration date? At a stock price of $65, the options would have been quite affordable and the profit on a $60 movement would have been a thing of beauty! Let's take a look.

A $60 strike price option purchased in January 2007, with an expiration date of January 2008, would have cost $13.82 or $1,382 for the contract of one hundred shares. Selling that contract on May 21, taking profits after only five months, rather than holding it for another six months, would have earned $61.20 per share or $6,120 for the contract of one hundred shares or $4,738 profit on our $1,382 investment. A whopping 440%.

This provides a wonderful example to demonstrate why we look for stocks with sound fundamentals that have gone through healthy pullbacks or down trending adjustment cycles or building base patterns, and then we jump on an option contract to ride them all the way up. When we are at the top of an upward trend as we are now in this stock, we can expect to reap smaller gains, but when the pendulum changes we're ready to jump off.

Again, let's take a look at TSO's chart below to view what happened over the next six months. If we had continued to watch this stock, what would we have seen? Did it ever give us a buy signal?

The first thing to note is that TSO's stock price is no longer in the $120 range. You see, on May 30, TSO split its stock shares, 2-to-1. Companies will split their stock shares as a way to raise cash. Stockholders end up with two shares for every share they held prior to the split. In a later chapter, we'll go into greater detail about trading stock splits, but for now just notice that the stock is now priced in the $60 range. Had we bought one option contract (one hundred shares) before the split, we would now have two contacts (two hundred shares).

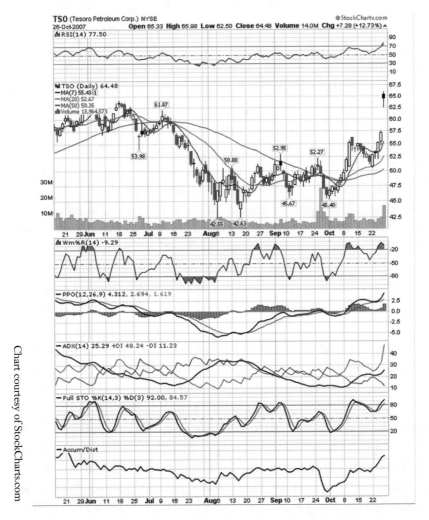

From the ending period of May 21 on the earlier chart, until June 25 on the chart, we can see that the stock zigzagged up and down, never giving a sound buy signal. While one indicator or another on June 13 showed a buy signal, the other indicators contradicted that information. Then on July 11, the price dropped to form a new pattern.

Note: You'll notice the squeeze that developed in August. The stock went up from $42.50 to $51 in seven days. That little squeeze would have produced a nice profit in a short period of time.

A put buy signal came on July 16. We could have made a nice profit riding the stock down from $57.50 to $45.

The next really clear call buy signal came on October 7 and 8. All indicators had crossed or were heading up. Fabulous profits would have been made for the move between $47.50 and $65, more than $2,000 profit on one option contract that expired in December. Not bad for an investment held less than a month!

Let's Look for More Opportunities

Clean Harbors, Inc. is a waste management company. Study its chart on page 108.

The RSI is running along, but below the 50 line (midrange). The candlesticks show us that in the second week in March something happened and the stock gapped down, after dropping from a near high in late February, following the trend of the overall stock market reversal. The bad news might have been poor earnings, a lawsuit, the loss of a contract, and so forth. If we care to know what happened, we easily look up the information.

At this point, the stock is still trying to recover from its lowest range. This could be an exciting stock. Because it has been down for some time, if it is ready to climb back up, as option traders we could enjoy a nice ride. But, do we know that its bout with tough times has ended? The quest for an answer could send us on the search for why this stock dropped in the first place.

So we looked it up and learned that Clean Harbors reported fourth quarter earnings that were up, but its outlook for the first quarter was down. Then, when it reported its first quarter earnings on May 9, its earnings were up, and they expected a better second quarter, but the stock dropped. Profit taking? A down day in the overall market?

We almost always advise not holding an option through earnings report dates because that's an unpredictable time, especially if you're holding a profit. If the situation with the company is volatile, then holding through this period could wipe out profits. (We'll discuss how to look up those earnings report dates in our chapter on option purchasing.)

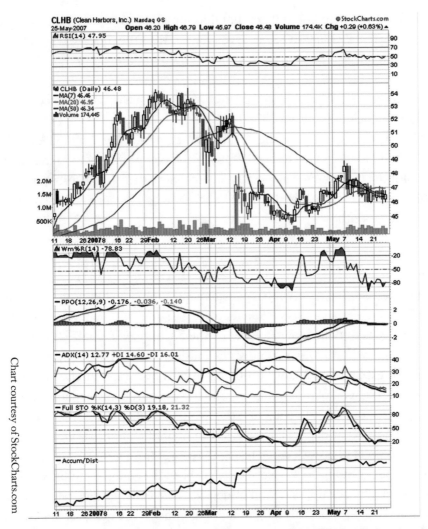

The Williams %R on this chart is in the oversold area, giving us room and time to earn a profit as it rises up to the overbought range.

If we were to draw one line over the top of the lower group of candlesticks, from March to May, and another line under the bottoms, we would see that it creates a horizontal channel. The area across the top of the candlesticks at $48.50 is a line of resistance (the ceiling). The stock has been bouncing back and forth between the floor and the ceiling for almost three months. It is going to take a powerful thrust to propel this stock above that line and to fill that gap created with the rapid drop on March 12. That thrust might be the next earnings report or some new contract. Its next earnings report will be in July or August of 2007. That seems a long time to wait for this stock to either inch up until that earnings date or to wait for it to gap up on a good report.

The PPO is at the zero line and running horizontal. Not much oomph. Notice the lines of the PPO and ADX that formed a squeeze in April. Though, as we would have expected, we see some upward movement as the ADX line pushed away, it never turned upward to begin a trend. The +DI line is now heading down and the –DI seems to be gaining strength. The Full STO is in the oversold range and doesn't yet appear to be ready to make a turn upward. The odd item thrown into this mix of information is the interest shown on the accumulation/distribution line. It's at a very high level and has been since the big drop in March. This makes us wonder if something is brewing under the surface that those of us on the outside are unable to see. Is this company a candidate for a merger or acquisition? It could be that the tutes are making small, regular purchases in anticipation of some bigger event.

Based on this chart, we would put this stock on a watch list to check daily. Once it got close to $48.50, we would be prepared to purchase an option when a breakout occurred beyond that point. In addition, you'll note that at this moment it's difficult to see how the moving averages line up. Is the blue on top or in the middle? At the point that a breakout might take place, all three moving averages would be locked together and heading upward. All three MAs consolidating in one place and all heading in the same direction seems to have a great deal of thrust power, which is another reason to keep a close eye and to be prepared to jump on when it happens.

Overall, Clean Harbors is a fundamentally sound company that projected a poorer than expected outcome that never occurred. Its indicators are all in the right places, but the stock could continue to bounce back and forth between resistance and support; if we purchased a contract now we'd tie up our money up for an unknown period of time. Yet, something seems to be brewing that deserves close attention. The move up to $51 and then $53 and beyond would be a big jump for this stock, well worth watching.

So, let's see what happened.

Clean Harbors stock hung out in the range of $47 until June 25. At this point we got clear buy signals and indicators crossed and the candlesticks closed above the 7-day SMA and the SMAs lined up in the order of an uptrend. On July 23, the RSI dropped and over the following days, all the other indicators followed the downward path.

Here is a case where we would close our long position, our call, and we could open a short position, a put, on the same stock. In hindsight, we see that we could have ridden it down from $53.83 to $42.52. We might have been shaken out of our put on August 27, as the candles started upward, but if we followed our signals of SMA crosses before selling, we would have held through this time and reaped the benefit of another $2 profit on our contract of one hundred shares or $200.

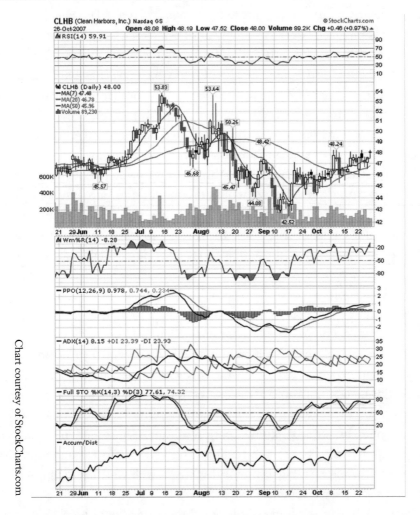

Chart courtesy of StockCharts.com

Looking at a Well-Known Company

You may not have heard of Cree or TSO or Clean Harbors, but you've no doubt heard of Marriott International, Inc., the lodging chain. A quick look at this chart tells us it's fallen on hard times. During the last week in April, it reported earnings with a downbeat forecast. Whether the market reacted

appropriately or over-reacted, who can say? Nonetheless, a price correction
is at hand.

The RSI is in the mid range and going lower, into oversold. The candlestick chart shows an adjustment of a $7 drop during the decline. It seems
as if some pattern is being formed. Could that be a cup and handle? We see
what might be the left side of a base. Bases should last no less than seven
weeks. This one, if a cup and handle formation is taking place, it is in the
fourth week, which would give another week or two across the bottom and
then a rise up, creating the right side.

The SMAs are in the order of a down trending stock, though the 7-day
SMA seems to be making attempts at crossing over the 20-day.

Williams %R is pointed downward from a mid-point, after rising from an oversold position. Its upward movement seems to have fizzled out. The PPO has just crossed, and its histogram has come into positive territory. The ADX, along with the PPO, has created a bit of a squeeze, yet the ADX line and the +DI have yet to turn in an upward direction. Though we have said that 98% of the time a squeeze will end in upward movement, none of the other indicators confirm this upward movement yet. The squeezing pressure will have to tighten before there is this upward pop. The full STO started to rise, touched the 50 line, but seems to be retreating.

Overall, this stock at some point in the coming weeks will be ripe and bound for higher lows. Yes, we will probably still see red (low) candles but they will be higher up (so that it creates a bottom and doesn't keep dropping lower); for the moment, however, it seems to be in a place of fermenting. Like wine, it takes time to become full bodied. We would put this stock on a list to check in a week or so, and then again a week later.

Let's see what happened to Marriott. Were we correct to wait? Did it form a base? What happened to the squeeze?

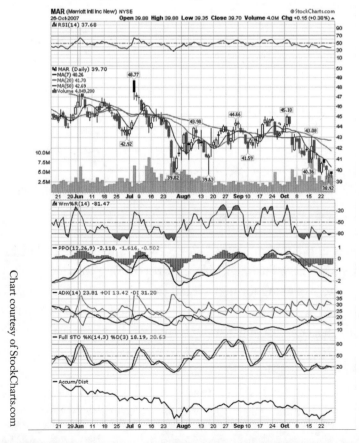

Chart courtesy of StockCharts.com

A completion of a base never really materialized. The SMAs, though they tried to line up in an uptrend formation, were never able to hold that alignment.

The squeeze on May 29 popped and started to spread apart, with four days of solid and high volume buying on the fifth day. On the sixth day, the pressure fizzled out and the stock began to drop to its former position. Even with the big jump on July 3, it couldn't hold its ground. That big black candle shows that though the bulls won the day with a great deal of buying, plenty of selling (profit taking) took place as it jumped in price.

Often when a stock has been down for a length of time, stockholders will jump for joy when a stock finally has a move up. They'll clap their hands, happy for any bit of profit, and just as happy to sell. It's as if they collectively exclaim, "I'm out of here. I'm done with this slow-mover! I broke even, or nearly so, and I count myself lucky."

We see another squeeze forming on the right side of this chart, but its history of short ups and downs doesn't make it as attractive as other squeezes on strong trending charts.

Baker Hughes (see chart below) supplies products and technology services to the oil and natural gas industries. It operates in two segments–drilling and evaluation, and completion and production. Like TSO, it has had a nice run up since mid-March and has recently had a pullback, so that now it's near its most recent high.

RSI is above 50 and just under the 70 point, leading to the overbought range. The fact that we are at the same high level on the candlesticks, yet the RSI is below the previous high, shows negative divergence. The candlesticks are at an area of resistance, sometimes called a double-top, which is a bearish pattern. Lets see what the other indicators show.

The Williams %R was rising out of an oversold position, but has stalled and gone horizontal.

The PPO has started to rise upward and is just below a cross, but seems to have flattened a bit. The histogram has not yet crossed the zero line. The ADX line could be about to curve upward, but would still be considered horizontal. The +DI is again horizontal and the –DI down.

Full STO is the most positive indicator, because it's crossed and passed the 50 line.

The accumulation/distribution line indicates a great deal of interest.

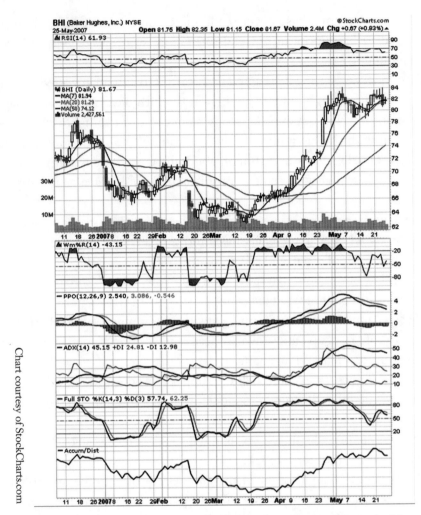

Settling back and taking all the indicators into consideration, this seems like it would be a good option candidate, but not a stock that will burst into the room in a frenzy. It very well may take a step back before it moves forward and up again.

What happened in the next six months?

Though the stock climbed in value from May 2 to June 18, it was an up and down tug of war. The Williams %R stair-stepped up, the PPO never did cross during that period. Its histogram stayed below the zero line. The ADX strength line trended down, showing that its thrust was losing momentum. The STO crossed back and forth numerous times. The accumulation and distribution showed that the institutes kept jumping in and out of the lunch line.

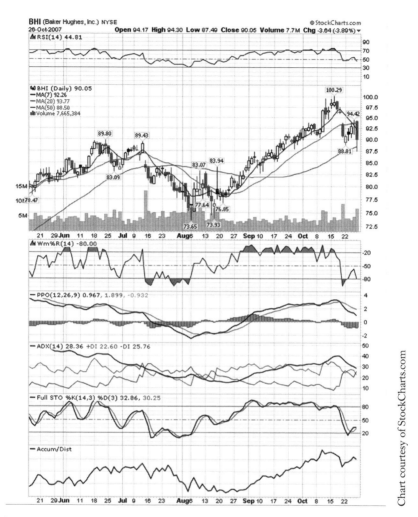

The month of August created a bullish pattern called a double bottom. The two points of the lows or the bottoms of a W pattern were within twenty-eight cents of each other. You might also decide that since the bottoms of the W are not pronounced, this is a misshapen cup. If that is the case, then you can see that it completed the cup, without a handle, in the area where it flattened out between September 1 and 17.

This is a good example of resistance. Note on the left side of this chart that the price twice tried to get above 90 and wasn't able to break through until it dropped and completed a pattern.

We'll say this now and repeat it again as we provide more examples– *price has memory*. Notice that the price flattened out at $87.50, the closest price below $90. On the left side, a great many people bought on July 14, and then a great many of those relieved buyers sold on August 16 when after three weeks, it finally got back up to that point.

So, then as I mentioned it flattened out and held for a bit around that same point between September 1 and 17, building up steam to burst through. When it finally broke through, it went up as high as $100.29. Notice, too, that when it dropped, it dropped to that point; on both September 22 and 26 it dropped and found support. The last candle hit the area of $87.50 and bounced back up like a trampoline. Price has memory!

Finally, on August 20, most of the indicators told us that a new uptrend was beginning, but it wasn't until the August 24 that the candlestick closed fully above the 7-day and 20-day SMAs, and not until September 1 did the SMAs line up in uptrending order.

Big risk takers might have purchased an option on BHI on August 20, standing ready to jump out if the situation reversed. Those preferring less risk would have purchased an option on the August 24 when signals were confirmed by the candle's close above the 7-day SMA. Those who go with the sure bet and lowest risk would have waited until the SMAs were in alignment. There was plenty of profit to be made at that point as it rose from $82.50 to $97.50.

A NASDAQ Stock

Many of the stocks we have discussed have been stocks on the Dow (stocks with three letters in their symbol), but ABFS is part of NASDAQ. It provides motor carrier transport services, which includes transporting general commodities, such as food and apparel. Earlier the COMPQ (NASDAQ Composite) chart that we showed for this period looked slightly more volatile in the last couple weeks, as also seen in ABFS' chart above.

On ABFS's chart, the RSI is in a mid-range, pointing upward. At first glance this stock appears to be in a wide channel. If we drew a line over the candlesticks at $42.50 and one under at $35 would we see that the price has been bouncing between these two levels, creating a channel for the last six months or so.

The Williams %R is up and just below twenty. By the cyclical pattern of the Williams %R, we might assume that the stock might rise from its

present price of $39.50 to $42 and then cycle back down, unless it breaks out. On April 25, it attempted to break out on high volume, but could not maintain that higher level (the tall black candle with the long upper shadow.) The next day it dropped back within the channel. We are at $39.36 at the end of the day of the last candle. In two and one half points, when it again reaches the top of our channel at $42.50, what will it do this time? That is the profit-raising question. A triple top if it reaches that point and stalls is a bearish pattern. Or will it have the oomph to break out this time?

The PPO is just before a cross above the zero line. The ADX line is horizontal with the +DI shadowing it; –DI is down, which shows the positive up movement is the stronger thrust. Full STO is at a mid-point, showing room for upward movement. Accumulation/distribution shows very little interest.

Overall, we would pass on this candidate for the moment. There are too many more great stock candidates out there that show stronger momentum. This one suggests it might stall around for awhile longer before it builds the drive to burst through the $42 resistance.

Let's see what happened. (See chart below.)

We made the right decision. ABFS did move up as far as $41 when the indicators crossed, but it stayed in the same channel until July, never gaining the strength to break out. Toward the end of July, it began to drop and continued to fall until it lost 25% of its value.

Qualifying the news that began this downward spiral, ABFS would have been a good put candidate. We discover this by weighing the importance of the change within the company. Was it a minor miscalculation or something

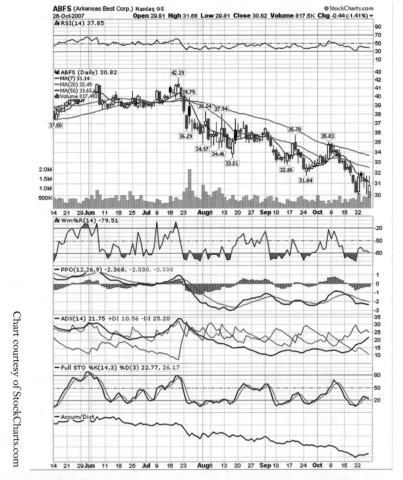

that will have a lasting impact on the company's bottom line? During the course of one day, July 23, the SMAs went from being aligned in an uptrend to a downtrend, as there was no space to speak of between the three SMA lines. When the price turned they all moved in tandem.

Looking at Another Sector

Carpenter Tech is involved in steel and iron alloys, including stainless steel.

RSI is below seventy, and between October 8 and 15, it was in a neutral, horizontal position, which reflects the previous six or so trading days. Then the stock started to turn up. During that neutral period, consolidation took place or a period of equal or near equal buying and selling that causes it to temporarily move against the trend.

Chart courtesy of StockCharts.com

The stock has been in a staggered uptrend since August 2007, making the right side of a cup pattern. The moving averages are all lined up in the proper order with 7-day above 20-day and 50-day as of the last candlestick. As long as this order is maintained, no matter the subtle adjustments in price, the overall movement will be up. The $125 price point has been a strong line of support.

Williams %R has just come into the overbought area, and based on assessing past patterns, once it reaches that area it could remain there for two or three weeks or longer. PPO is well above zero and has just crossed upward, and its histogram has made its first square above the zero. ADX line is bending up and the +DI has just crossed the black ADX strength line, while the –DI is heading south. Full STO is in the upper region, but has yet to level out. There is renewed interest seen on the accumulation/distribution indicator. Overall, this stock gives signals that it has more upward momentum.

This stock appears to be a good candidate for an option purchase at least up to the old high of $148. At that point, creating a double-top may result in another pullback before breaking out to new highs and the next leg up.

Looking at ETFs and the Option Index

Let's look at an option index and an ETF, the two other types of securities we've mentioned throughout this book. So far, in this chapter we've discussed stocks, which by their nature are more volatile and subject to fluctuations caused by earnings reports and other public relations issues. But when we examine an index and an ETF, you will see that their indicators can be read in the same manner as stocks.

QQQQ is an Index for the top one hundred stocks on the NASDAQ. Its numbers go up and down based on the composite performance of those one hundred stocks. There are composite Indexes for the Dow (DIA), Russell (RUT) and S&P (SPY).

The RSI is showing negative divergence. Although on May 21, the Index was at a high, the RSI value was lower, foretelling the change to come. On the last trading day we see an inkling of a reversal at the RSI fifty mark.

The candlesticks show one positive candle after two longer negative, selling candles. The 7-day MA is nearly touching the 20-day MA. It could easily drop through the 20-day on the next trading day. The second red candlestick closed below the 20-day MA, as did the last positive candle. The next line of support will be the 50-day MA if the market goes into a period of correction.

Williams %R confirms this positive turn upward, yet the PPO has not yet recrossed the red line, nor has the histogram moved above zero. The

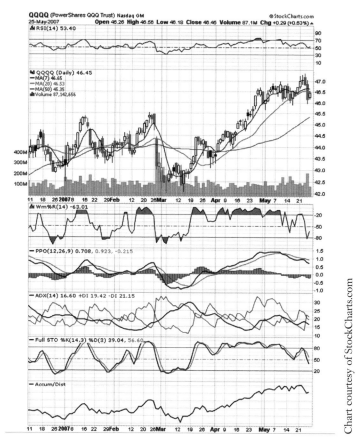

ADX line is waffling and the positive and negative DI lines are snaking around each other. The STO does not yet show the signs of a turn upward that the others are reflecting. The accumulation/distribution also seems to be trying to make up its mind.

As we said, this is an index comprised of one hundred NASDAQ stocks, and as you will recall with the overall Indices' charts listed at the beginning of this chapter, the market as a whole has been going through a time of adjustment. This chart's contradicting information would give us reason to hold off until we were sure of the market's trend.

Let's see what the future held here.

From May 21 through the first week in June, the Qs climbed $1.50 or so, and on into July formed a small channel, weaving back and forth between $46.50 and $48. In July, it climbed upward reaching $51.50, and then dropped to form a base. This $4 movement over the course of two months shows that we were right to hold off purchasing an option. A put buy signal was initiated on July 25, with the red candle close below the 7-day MA. The put would have been sold on August 16, as signaled by the red candle with

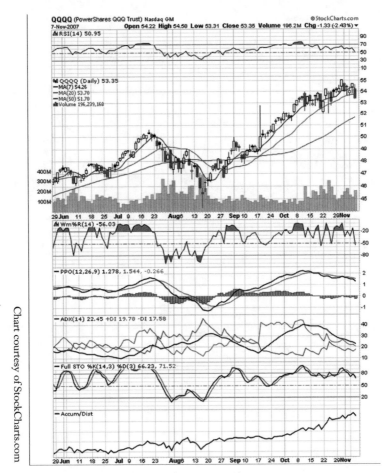

Chart courtesy of StockCharts.com

the long tail (a signal of change). On September 17, it completed the right side of the base and started a new leg upward.

An ETF

XLE is a composite of stock of energy-related companies. At first glance we see that this ETF has been in an uptrend since mid-March. The RSI shows healthy periodic pullbacks to the 7-day and 20-day MA, finding support and reversing. Profit taking during the course of an uptrend is the natural order of the market.

After the pullback (the last red candle) would be a great time to purchase an option. It is advantageous to purchase after a pullback because you are buying at a lower dollar point and can assume that it might quickly rise to that old high and beyond.

The SMAs are lined up in the order of an uptrend. Williams %R confirms that the ETF is again moving toward the overbought area. PPO has recently

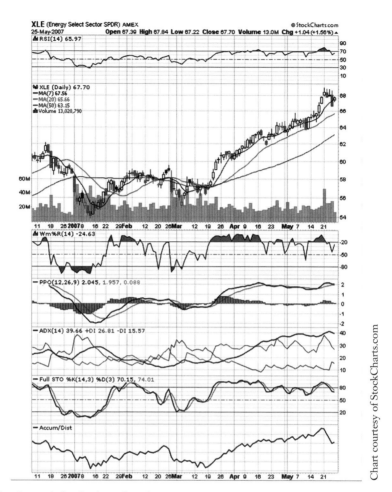

Chart courtesy of StockCharts.com

snaked back and forth, but for the moment is in positive territory on the histogram. The ADX reflects upward momentum and +DI rules the day. STO, too, is retracing up to overbought.

Overall, this energy ETF is in a good place for purchasing an option contract. We would not be getting in on the beginning of the up-trend, but providing it continues on this upward road for the next few weeks, there would be profit to be made.

Let's see how it continued to perform.

For the next seven weeks, XLE continued its upward path, going from $68 to $74. During the week of July 23, it pulled back and dropped below the 50-SMA to begin forming a pattern.

Note all the indicators that predicted this downward movement:

• Williams %R dropped out of the overbought area.

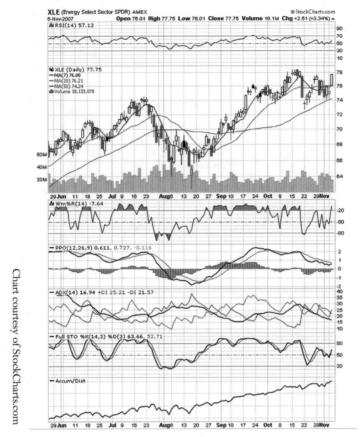

- The PPO line crossed downward and the histogram dropped below the zero line.

- The ADX +DI line crossed below the black strength line and the –DI.

- The –DI line moved upward, showing the trend was now bearish.

- From July until the end of August, the black ADX line flattened somewhat until it started to form a squeeze. The squeeze developed, and when the pressure built it pushed away forming the right side of the base pattern, beginning a new uptrend.

These charts and the analysis are included in order to help you gain experience and note trends for yourself. Come back to them as often as you need to in order to become familiar with the picture they show—and the messages they deliver.

Now that we have discussed possible buy signals, in the next chapter, we will look at sell signals.

Chapter Eight

RECOGNIZING SELL SIGNALS

Simply put, knowing when to sell is as important as knowing when to buy. We have both entry and exit strategies. Since we've looked at what and when to buy, we need to examine when to sell an option. We recommend that you learn and apply the rules for selling, and then develop the discipline to put the rules into practice over the long term. Briefly, an effective *exit strategy* must satisfy one of these three key elements:

1.   the upside is not limited from further growth;

2.   the loss is cut short; or,

3.   the profit is protected.

The 30-Day Rule

Plan to sell your option contract with thirty days left on your option. You do this to preserve the *time value* that is left. Each day into its current expiration month, a certain amount of value will drop off. Because of the effect of time value erosion on option premiums, particularly in the final weeks of the options life, you must be cognizant of this decay. So, no matter if your position is up or down, you should plan to close it—push the *close to sell* button.

The 7-Day Rule

Once you're in a trade, if the premium doubles, put the following 7-day rule into effect; if after doubling your cost, a daily closing price falls below the 7-day SMA in your call (long) position or above the 7-day SMA in a put (short) trade, close the position by selling your option. This rule can also be applied in choppy markets.

The 7% Rule

If after purchasing an option the underlying stock drops 7%, then it's time to sell. A winning option investor cuts losses quickly. It's the only way to protect yourself against a much larger loss. If you allow a loss to reach 20%, it will take a 25% gain to break even. If you wait longer and it goes down 25%, it will take 33% to break even. As we said before, develop strict discipline and follow your selling rules–and this process starts when you buy.

When you purchase an option contract, record it in your notebook and include the reasons you chose the stock in the first place. Then note the stock's current price and the price at which you would sell if it turned and never increased.

For example, if the stock had a $105 price, then you would note a 7% sell price of $97.65 or an overall loss of $7.35. One day it might lose $2.35 and you hold through that thinking it is a natural pullback. The next day the market is down and your stock drops another $2.95. If on the next subsequent days, with up and down movement your stock drops another $2.05 or more, push the sell button. In other words, we put the 7% rule in place when you buy–the rule is part of your thinking in making the transaction in the first place.

Wise Option Traders Remember
Take your losses quickly and take your profits slowly.

If after another few days the stock rights itself, you can purchase it again. The loss you experience will hurt, but you have lived to trade another day. Better to cut a loss short than hope that it will recover and end up losing even more.

Small losses are cheap insurance. In fact, small losses are the only insurance you can buy on your options.

Sell Signals–Calls

Use daily charts to determine sell signals.

- Determine where resistance is, and be prepared to sell if once it hits that area it pulls back.

- Wait for overbought conditions, then a dip, or a double-dip below the –20 on Williams %R or below the eighty on Stochastics.

- If the underlying's price goes up and then drops 5%–10%, take your profits and get out of the kitchen–it's getting too hot.

- If the value of your option declines by 50%, cut your losses and get out.

- If the option doubles in value, and then there is a close below the 7-day SMA, take your profits.

- Once Stochastics moves above seventy, be watchful and prepared to sell, confirmed by other signals.

- When PPO histogram bars get shorter and flatten out, and that line crosses over and above the PPO line, it is time to get out.

We've already pointed out a truism of the trading business, but it bears repeating: *fear travels twice as fast as greed.*

We need to remember this and keep it at the forefront of our minds. A fall in a stock's price (selling off) happens fast. Investors become afraid of losing their profits or losing their investment, so the selling (fear) eventually becomes a fire, where investors throw their stocks into the blaze and run. Once the fire is out, the climb back up is slow and steady, step by step. Once you have plodded up the trend mountain, be watchful, spot the signs of reversals, and get out while you have profits in hand. You can't lose money taking a profit.

Look at the *weekly chart* to get a broader view of what is happening with the stock, index, or ETF.

Does the weekly chart agree and confirm what is seen on the daily chart, or is the daily chart experiencing a temporary blip down in what would otherwise be a continued uptrend?

Sell Signals–Puts

Use the daily charts.

- Determine where support is and be prepared to sell once it reaches that point and appears not to be moving through it or reverses.

- Wait for oversold conditions, a spike or double spike above the –80 on Williams %R or a turn and rise above twenty on Stochastics.

- If the underlying's price value goes down and then rises 5%–10%, take your profits and get out of the heat.

- If the option doubles in value, and then a candle closes above the 7-day SMA, take your profits.

- Once Stochastics's black line moves below thirty, be watchful and prepared to sell, confirmed by other signals.

- When PPO histogram bars are getting short and flattening out, and red line crosses over and below the PPO (black) line, it is time to say farewell.

- If the value of your option declines by 50%, cut your losses and get out.

Looking at *weekly charts,* you'll get a broader view of what is happening with the stock, index, or ETF. Does the weekly chart agree and confirm what you see in the daily chart, or is the daily chart experiencing a blip up in what would otherwise be a continuation of the downward trend?

The Technical Analysis

Technical analysis provides a window into the psychology of the market. While no crystal ball exists, technical analysis can be a tool in your trading kitchen drawer, always available to help you put probabilities on your side.

In addition, you must remember that trading is not a world filled with absolutes! We can't provide the perfect trading system because there is no such thing. However, despite the lack of certainty and absolutes, through practiced chart reading, we can determine and see many of these probabilities taking shape before they come to fruition.

Let's say that we're working with an option contract on Deere, the tractor company. We had purchased an April call option contract on January 12, 2007, so we would be watching for signals to sell before mid-March, or thirty days prior to expiration.

During January and February three candlesticks closed below the 7-day MA, but we were still early in the contract and the other indicators (ADX, STO, A/D) said we were still in an uptrend. Then, on February 27, a big overall market correction took place, and this is where we would have sold, protecting our profit.

But, you say, by the middle of March it had nearly regained its price. True, but we would not and could not have known this.

If we had purchased a call option on April 16, after the decline in price and reversal up, we would have closed this position on April 28, when the price closed below the 7-day MA. We could have decided to repurchase a contract on May 3, when it again closed over the 7-day MA, and would have sold this position on May 16.

If you run your eye down the indicators between the week of May 14 to May 21, you will see that some of the indicators gave warning as early as May 15, and another as late as May 21. This is how it often is: one or two indicators provide hints, and we can make a choice based on those, or we can wait for further confirmation. Ultimately, you will choose the sell indicators that you like to work with best and will come to rely on them.

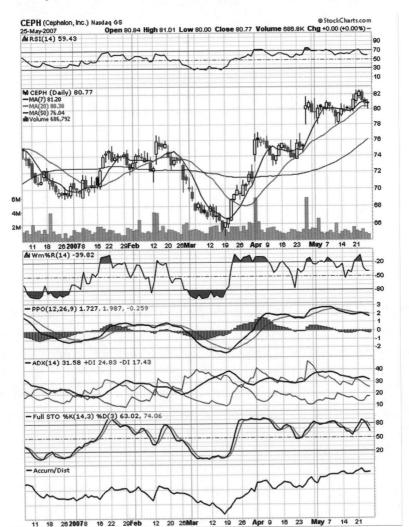

Chart courtesy of StockCharts.com

These closing positions would also have been opportunities to purchase put options contracts. If we had bought a put on Feb 27, we would have sold on March 3, as the indicators rose up on Williams %R and STO. The circumstances would have been similar the last week in March and April. If we purchased a Put contract on May 16, we would consider selling that contract on the next trading day after the last day shown on the chart.

On the chart on page 130, we see a wonderful put purchasing opportunity on February 20, and then selling the position on March 20.

However, unless the market as a whole is experiencing a downward adjustment for an extended period of time, it's unusual to purchase a put (short) that lasts as long as a month. We would have considered making this put purchase when the first candle closed below the 7-day SMA, and then we would have sold when the RSI, Williams %R, STO came off their low positions. We also draw your attention to the *squeeze* that preceded the upward movement in March. If we had bought on that squeeze, we would have sold on April 10, when the price closed below the 7-day SMA, even though only a couple of the other indicators confirmed that earliest sell signal.

Clear versus Cloudy Thinking

At times it seems as if the indictors are much clearer as to when to get into an option contract than when to get out. This isn't really the case and the indicators are clear both ways. However, once we've purchased a contract and have realized a profit, our vision becomes blurred by greed. We wonder if we can't squeak out a few more dollars before selling.

The blurring can be even more threatening if the signal is given, but thus far, we have not realized the profit we expected. Again, our vision becomes clouded–we fight the signal, rationalizing why we shouldn't give up now and take this small loss, when there is every reason to think that it might reverse, might go back up. With this cloudy vision, we fight, and we drag our feet, until the next day, the loss that would have been digestible now becomes a mouthful that we are truly unable to swallow. Before we know it we are choking on a loss that is half our contract investment. Then, without another thought, we sell, and so it is that we survive to trade another day. We see our mistake in retrospect and learn to never let a dish burn us twice.

The bottom line here is to follow the total analysis of the indicator signals, placing the weight on the ones that indicate change–and then we act on what the majority tell us. We've heard it a hundred times and have said it ourselves, "Well, I thought…"

But, *the market doesn't care what we think.* We can't out think the market. All we can do is follow the pack, reading and analyzing the signal-tracks they leave.

Chapter Nine

SETTING UP
A TRADING ACCOUNT

Perhaps you've been paper trading for a while now (specific paper trading details are discussed in Chapter Twelve), and you believe you're ready to set up a trading account. Taking this step allows you to *virtually trade,* which means that you can navigate and become familiar with the site, select options from the chains, and push the buy and sell buttons, trading without money. Remember that you don't need to fund an account when you open it.

As you know, many online brokerage houses are available, including *optionsXpress, Ameritrade, TradeStation, Tradeking,* and *Investrade.* For our purposes here, we'll use optionsXpress.com. For your convenience, there is a link to optionsXpress on our website, WomenOptionTraders.com, and mention WomenOptionTraders as your referral source. OptionsXpress has received favorable ratings with option traders and its site is easy to use. Once you open an account, you can practice virtual trading without transferring money into your account.

Without question, virtual trading is a fabulous way to experience trading without risk. This can be carried out in a few ways. For example, the site keeps track of all of your trading activity. Many women trade virtually in addition to trading with real funds. Why would they do this? Perhaps they have an instinct about a stock's chart, but they're not ready to risk a real money investment. But with virtual trading, they can act on intuition and trade, thereby gaining experience investing in trades that may be beyond her current financial means.

Following the Steps

Okay, again using optionsXpress as an example, note the following:

- First go to www.optionsXpress.com and click on *Open an Account*. From there, you will be taken through a fairly straightforward online application.

- You will be asked to choose a *cash* or a *cash/margin account*. *Margin trading* operates on a line of credit and is not something we neither do nor recommend for the beginning trader.

- At the end of the application, you will be asked to print out, sign, and mail your application to optionsXpress. There is a place to create a free FedEx overnight shipping label. It may take several days to receive and validate your application. (In contrast, Ameritrade, allows you to sign up online, but the application process is much lengthier.)

- OptionsXpress also asks if you want to trade stock as well as options. We recommend checking *yes* on that box. While it doesn't happen often, now and then a lower price stock is so inexpensive that there is little difference between the cost to purchase a few shares of stock and what an option might be. Here, too, Ameritrade asks more complex questions regarding *covered calls* (which means you must own the underlying security) and other choices. Since we're keeping things simple, we confine discussion and our activity to trading options.

Other Issues

You will see warnings and caveats on these sites, because each brokerage house wants to be certain that you understand the risks. These companies are not responsible for your choices or any losses you incur through the use of their investing tools and services.

We suggest you paper trade and trade virtually, entering and exiting trades, until you feel confident and ready to invest for real, whether that's six months or even a year from now. You can engage in virtual trading once you open an account (since you don't need to fund it), but you can paper trade and get a feel for it before becoming involved in virtual trading. Whether you trade on paper, virtually, or with real money, trading experience is trading experience.

When you are ready to fund your account, you can do one of the following.

1. Mail a check or money order. (Brokerage houses don't accept credit card checks.)

2. Wire the funds.

3. Use electronic transfer of funds (ACH). If you want the firm to initiate this, you need to set this service up in advance at your bank.

Example

For an account with optionsXpress, this is what you need to do.

- You set up ACH on a checking or savings account at your bank in the same name as your optionsXpress account.

- You give this ACH information to optionsXpress, and they then will do a security procedure in which they make a small deposit and small withdrawal (usually under $1.00) from your account to verify that the numbers are correct. They will ask you to verify the amounts of these transactions to be certain that you are who you say you are, and that you really have access to the bank account.

- Then, if you have set up online banking, you can check your bank account to report the amounts deposited and withdrawn back to optionsXpress. If you don't have online banking capability, then you'll call your bank to verify the transaction. OptionsXpress will send the email giving an all-clear signal, allowing you to initiate the transfer of funds to them, thereby funding the account with whatever amount of money you choose.

- After the funds have been received by optionsXpress, there is a three-day clearance period before the funds are available to be used for trading.

- You use this easy and convenient ACH capability to add funds to your trading account or transfer profits back to your checking or savings account.

Once your account is open and you trade with real money, optionsXpress acknowledges each option purchase or sale with an email confirming the details of the transaction. At the end of the month, optionsXpress sends out a statement of account activity, similar to a checking account bank statement.

Virtual Trading

Just to review, *virtual trading* is *simulated* trading—you get all the excitement, but take no risk because you aren't actually investing any money. Again we stress practice, practice, and practice some more by virtual trading until you are confident about when to enter and exit your trades.

To begin virtual trading on optionsXpress, go to *login* (upper right), and after typing in your login name and password information, hold the cursor on the *Toolbox* tab, click on *Virtual Trade,* and then click the *Launch Virtual Trade.* At this point, you'll set up a virtual account, which is based on the information given in your regular account. You will see that $5,000 of virtual funding is placed in your account. There is a tab at the top to add additional funds if you choose.

Once in the Virtual Trade space do the following.

1.   Click on *option* rather than stock or covered-calls, and so forth.

2.   Enter the *symbol* of the underlying security upon which you are seeking information.

3.   Click on *chains.*

4.   Choose the option you wish to purchase and click *trade.*

5.   You will be asked what action to take.

   □ If you are buying, then in the drop down box select buy to open.

   □ Then, when you are ready to sell select sell to close.

   As explained earlier, option contracts are sold in quantities of one hundred. If you purchase one contract, you are buying the option on 100 shares of the underlying security. If you purchase two contracts, it is on 200 shares.

6.   The next box you'll address is: *market order* or *limit order.*

Market orders trade at the current market price, which should be very close to the price that will show on the options chain screen. If you are trading during market hours (Wall Street hours, and therefore, eastern standard time), there shouldn't be any unexpected surprises. However, the market often trades quickly in a hot market where a stock price moves up and down within seconds. Option prices change a little more slowly, but as you click *place order* the option could go up or down a nickel or dime. The sale happens in seconds.

With a *limit order,* you are specifying at what price you want to trade, and the duration (trading day) they should *float* the order, that is, try to fill it at the price you requested. If the market never reaches the price you specified during that period of time, the order will be canceled. This strategy can be useful if you are going to be away, but it is not nearly as beneficial as actually being there to take advantage of current events.

Why and How Would You Use a Limit Order?

Suppose you're leaving the house before the market opens and you know that you will not get back until the end of the day. Earlier, before this particular morning, you found a stock on which you want to purchase an option and it closed last night with an option price of $2.25. As you were getting dressed this morning, the crawl across the TV screen said the stock was moving higher during the pre-hours. Of course, by now you know that the market often jumps and is high first thing as it opens, and then settles back late morning and around lunch.

You want to buy two contracts, but rather than place a market order to be filled soon after the market opens (when it might be filled at $2.75 on the initial jump), you place a *limit order* for $2.15. Your thinking behind this is that after the initial hoopla of morning activity wanes, the market is apt to slide back or, perhaps, during lunch hour, even drop below its opening price.

Once you get home and check the computer, two things might have happened.

1. One, it was a strong market day and the stock never dropped down to your price of $2.15, so your order was never filled.

2. Two, your order was filled at the price you set and by handling it this way you saved–which means you earned–an extra sixty cents on each share or $60 on each of the two contracts. This is a total of $120 on the two hundred shares more than you would have made if the contract had been filled at $2.75.

    In addition, as the stock climbed back up to $3 by the end of the day, you made another twenty-five cents per share or a total of $170 for the day ($3 less $2.15 = 85 cents times 200 shares). The contract at the market price of $2.75 would have made a total of $50 for the day ($3 less $2.75 = 25 cents times 200 shares = $50.)

That said, we generally recommend sticking to *market orders* because you are there watching and the variance when the contract is actually filled might be a few cents to a dime.

On the other hand, we advise against placing an *open to buy* market order while the market is closed. After-hours trading happens in foreign exchanges and in ways we are not privy to; therefore, in the morning, there might be an unexpected transaction. At the time you placed your market order, say in the wee hours of the night or early morning, you think you are making a purchase at $3.20 per share and when you check your account, because after-hour activity sent this stock up, you have paid $5.40 per share.

Market orders also work in reverse. Let's say you decide to purchase an option that has an ask price of $4. If the stock drops while you are placing your transaction and the ask price drops in that minute or two to $3.80, your order will be filled at $3.80, which is the price the market was asking at the moment that it was filled.

You are always asked to preview the order, and be sure to do so. You preview an order to be certain that you have the right underlying security and correct strike price, expiration month, and quantity. When you're satisfied that the information is correct, you place the order, which serves as the conformation.

The *order status* tab will advise you where your option order is at the moment—*pending, filled, canceled.*

Virtual trading has advantages over paper trading. For example, you get a chance to practice going through the exact motions of placing trades, becoming familiar with the trading screens, and sidestepping any errors you might be prone to make.

The table you previously used to track your paper trades is now created for you by optionsXpress. Find it by clicking the *Activity* tab across the top of the virtual account screen.

The same procedures apply to placing trades with real money. Once you begin to virtual trade and are comfortable with the screens, we suggest you investigate other screens available through optionsXpress or other brokerage firms.

You will find net gains or losses, including commission paid on your trade, under *Analysis* on the virtual account screen. Remember no real funds are used while virtual trading, but it simulates all the procedures in an actual trade.

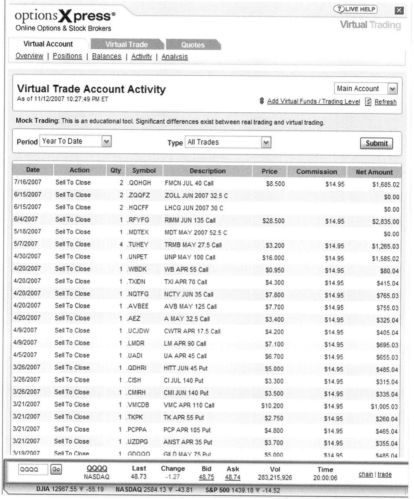

Using Other Tools

Many women want to keep their trading procedures simple and have the steps down pat. These women don't want to complicate the issue. But, other women want many tools at their disposal. You may not yet know where you fit along the spectrum, and you may change as you become more confident.

If you click on an *underlined security symbol* on a chain or chart page, it will bring up information about that company or index. On that page, the news tab will bring up headlines or articles similar to those available at finance.yahoo.com.

One of the extra tools is *Streaming Quotes,* which means you can watch the security's price change second by second. You'll find this tool under the *Quotes* tab. You'll see *Streaming* and then you'll click the green box that launches streaming quotes (on the right side). To initiate this you must have or install Java (optionsXpress takes you through the steps to install this program). Once you have streaming quotes functioning, you type in the symbols of the stocks or indexes you want to watch. These can be added or deleted as your interest dictates.

The first symbol typed starts your list, and each subsequent symbol follows, so your most recent entry appears at the bottom of the list. However, the next time you come to streaming quotes the symbols will be in alphabetical order, having been automatically rearranged in that order.

Whether you actually use the information or not, streaming is a fascinating process to watch, and gives you a view of the way stocks tick up and down as the buy and sell orders occur. There are some times when hot stocks, ones in the news or responding to news events or earnings reports, will start moving before hours. These are the stocks you'll often see crawl across the TV screen in the morning, and you can watch the pre-market quotes streaming in the half-hour or so before the market opens, when the pre-market activity is shown. This can give you an inkling of how the morning trades will go.

Other Features at OptionsXpress

You can receive email price alerts once you incur a certain percentage of profit or loss, which can alert you to times to buy or sell.

A tool called *trailing stops* allows optionsXpress to automatically close your position when a certain dollar amount or percentage loss has occurred. These are safeguards to protect you from unexpected circumstances, especially if you are expecting to be away from the computer for an extended period of time. If you're away on business or taking a dream vacation, it's usually better to close positions with a profit than risk experiencing a drop, at which point the broker acts on a stop.

Trailing Stops and the Issue of Emotion

Trailing stops have advantages, the most important of which is that it takes the emotions out of closing a losing position. In Chapter 8, we mentioned using the *7% rule*–closing an option when the stock's price is down 7% from the point you purchased the option, thereby limiting your loss. However,

7% of a stock's price doesn't always equate to 7% of the option price because of the other variables involved in option pricing (discussed later).

Nonetheless, it is always a good idea to fix an amount in your mind that is the lowest bid price you will accept, after which you will sell. For example, we mentioned the *50% rule*–if you lose 50% of your investment, close the option immediately, preserving the balance of your funds.

The *save order* function is a handy tool that allows you to select the options you would like to purchase or sell, fill out the order form, and then save them so they are ready for the right moment to initiate the transaction. Using this tool saves time when you are watching and trying to act on a stock's lowest or highest price to initiate a buy or sell order. The order has the symbol and action term set and is ready for you to push the order button.

OptionsXpress Charts

OptionsXpress provides charting capabilities on their site. To use them, go to the main heading *Quotes* and then select *Charts*. This screen provides a choice between *Xpress charts,* which is a basic chart for quick reference, *Java charts,* a step up with streaming prices, or, near the heading, you can select the *Beta Flex charts.* The *Beta Flex charts* allow for much of the flexibility available on StockCharts.com, such as changing the time frame and adding indicators and oscillators. This is done under their heading of *upper and lower studies.* On the left side you can select the *streaming* setting, and it will give you moment by moment current prices, reflected on the last candle. Under the tab select tool you can draw in *trend lines* and *channels.* In addition, on this page you can click on the *underlined security's symbol,* and it will bring you to specific information on that company.

The easiest way to discover the possibilities of these pages is to go exploring and see for yourself what information you find useful. Jot down a few notes in the beginning of your explorations so that you can find your way back to that information until that trail becomes familiar to you.

Option Charts

OptionsXpress offers a chart on the option itself, which is something not available anyplace else that we've seen. To access these charts, go to the main heading, *Quotes,* and then click on *chains.* Once you've found an option for which you'd like to see a chart, click on the *underlined option symbol.* That brings you to a page with information about that particular option.

Here, you'll see another selection of headings across the middle. Click *charts,* and again you have a choice of *Xpress charts, Java charts,* or *Beta Flex charts.* The Beta Flex charts on the specific option allows for the addition of indicators and oscillators, change in time frames, and drawing tools.

Again, we suggest exploring, and during that process, you'll discover a smaller chart called *Volatility View.* (The next chapter covers these charts and volatility in general.)

You'll also see the heading *Historical Quotes.* Under either the chains or charts page, Historical Quotes will list the open, high, low, and close prices and volume for each day over the last few months for either the security or the option. This information is particularly interesting when it comes to a specific option, because its price history is not known or reflected on the candlestick. In general, we know that it would have gone up or down based on the price movement of the underlying instrument, but the historical information gives a dollar amount of the option's price movement.

An option that has dropped in price will often rise back up to its old high within a few days. This table helps to project over a short period of time what the option's price movement might be. This, too, depicts the span of price change over the course of a day, which can help decide where to set a stop order, if you chose to set one, by going a smidge beyond its normal daily swing in price.

Getting the Help You Need

You will see that optionsXpress lists its phone number on its website, and it has technicians on hand ready to answer questions about opening an account or using their site. In addition, you'll see a *live help* button in the right hand corner. Clicking on it brings up a live chat box, where you can type your question and receive an immediate answer.

OptionsXpress will *not* provide trading advice. This firm doesn't operate as a broker who advises clients. All traders–whether purchasing the securities themselves or options on an underlying security–should make informed decisions based on their own careful research of the securities' past performance and expected movement.

Chapter Ten

VOLATILITY

Volatility is like a shadow that affects option pricing (briefly explained here), but also affects the strength of the security's movement. Many volumes have been written on volatility and yet few investors understand its significance. In decades past, it was rare that one of the major indices changed in value by 2% in a single day–maybe it occurred once or twice a year at most. In the last few years, this equates to a $100–$200+ move in one day on the Dow.

During the summer and autumn of 2007, $100+ swings in the Dow happened more than two dozen times. During October and November of 2007, those $100 shifts were a daily occurrence. Therefore, it has become a subject that deserves greater attention and understanding.

Volatility is important to us as option traders because we're interested in the direction the market moves, but beyond that, how big the move is over a certain period of time. In other words, we're interested in the volatility of the market. We want to understand the underlying's (the stock's) tendency to fluctuate sharply and regularly.

Volatility levels rise when the overall market shoots up and when it drops dramatically. We see and feel volatility during periods of fever-pitched buying and selling and frantic changes in supply and demand. Market makers take volatility into account in their option pricing.

Volatility is the *only* variable to go into option pricing and it is subjective. The other factors of the premium's price are known: the stock's price, strike price, days to expiration (time), and risk-free rate of return.

As a generality, higher-priced stocks tend to be less volatile than lower priced stocks. If all other things were equal, the security with the highest volatility would have the highest price options. Hence, the more volatile a security or the overall market, the larger than normal price swings, and the more money an investor can gain or lose in a short period of time.

Volatility is measured in two ways–*historical volatility* and *implied volatility*.

- *Historical volatility* is measured using past data, covering any period we desire–10 days, 20 days, 50 days, and 100 days are common time frames.

- *Implied volatility* is an attempt by traders and market makers to assess the future volatility of the underlying instrument or security. It's a guesstimate.

The *higher* the implied volatility, the greater the possibility the underlying asset will move in your favor. The *lower*, more stagnant the implied volatility, the lower the possibility it will move in your favor. The higher the implied volatility, the more expensive the option becomes because of the greater possibility that it will end up in your favor and yield greater profit.

Time and volatility change the price of an underlying security in the same way. The more time, the more likely a big change will occur. We are also able to say, the greater the volatility, the more likely a big change will occur. But these two conditions do not necessarily coincide.

Using Volatility

Once you choose an option, check the stock and option's volatility by looking at the *Volatility View* at optionsXpress. This chart shows both historic and implied volatility.

Look at the historical value, given a number and a line on the graph. This is the volatility at which the option is normally priced. If the implied volatility is higher than this, the premium is apt to be 5%, 10%, or 15% up from normal. In addition, the spread between the bid and the ask price will be larger. This adds to the amount that the stock price will have to move in your option's direction before you see any profit.

The only time it is okay to delve into this high pricing formula is if your intention is to buy high and sell even higher. Let's say you see that a stock is apt to jump further over a short-short period of time–or is apt to drop even further in the case of a put–and you choose to purchase an option based on that guesstimate. You must then watch the option closely and give yourself time to get out while the price is still high.

Other than the example above, it's best to purchase options when the implied volatility has peaked, meaning the stock is ready to rally. So, under normal circumstances, you'll buy when the historical and implied volatilities are closer in agreement, meaning the option is price based on volatility that is closer to its normal range.

Chart courtesy of optionsXpress.com

On the chart above, the underlying's stock price is the shaded area.

One line is the *historic volatility* and the other is the *implied volatility*. If the implied volatility is *lower* than the historical, it is a contrary indicator, meaning that you could expect a security explosion. This low volatility is caused by over-complacency, and the market explodes in one direction or the other and shakes things up. Low volatility creates low-priced options, but, remember, they can move in either direction. Nonetheless, it's noteworthy if daily implied volatility substantially differs from the historical. You would then use other indicators to try to predict its direction.

The chart for the Qs doesn't show any significant areas where the implied volatility is lower than the historic, though it does have some spikes in the implied volatility where the option prices would have been priced higher, having a broader gap between the ask and bid price.

On the next chart for RIMM, we checked out October 5, where we see the large spike in implied volatility. That day RIMM's stock jumped $13 on a trading volume of 65 million shares. On October 4, we saw a volume of 35 million shares and a $4 price move, a total of $17 for the two days. The week prior had a consistent number of days at 18 million shares with a $1 or $2 change.

Based on this steady movement during the weeks prior to October, the implied volatility was below the historic. Eventually, the historic average

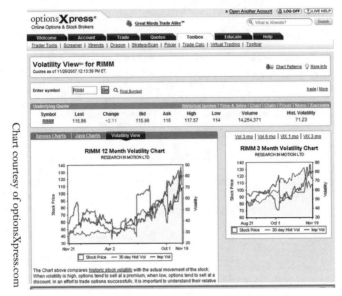

Chart courtesy of optionsXpress.com

fell, as high-volume days dropped from the beginning of its calculation period and lower-volatility days were added. Then a change took place. This change was caused by news of RIMM's earnings, reported on October 4, after the market closed. Maybe, on October 4, there were whispers of a good report in the marketplace and the price began to climb in anticipation of the report. The good numbers shook things up and the implied volatility shot up on the increased volume. Over the next couple days as the excitement waned, the implied volatility fell back in place, closer to the historic level. It stayed there until the second week in November when RIMM's price dropped and implied volatility again rose, thus creating a wider ask-bid spread on the purchase of put options.

Expert chart-reading comes into play anytime you examine a chart and evaluate indicators. The indicators tell us when stocks have become over-sold or overbought. We note the eminent crosses of the MADC or PPO and ADX. We consider what the divergences–positive or negative–might be predicting. Then we buy our options at a low price before the big move, before the implied volatility jumps. Then we sell before the next big change or at a high bid price when the implied and historic volatility are realigned.

Overall Market Volatility Chart

The *CBOE Volatility Index,* known as the VIX, is an index indicator that reflects the volatility of the overall market.

The VIX chart can be difficult to comprehend. It runs the opposite of the

S&P 100 and has been called the *fear index*. To illustrate, if you look at the chart and interpret it to mean that the VIX will be moving up, you are then betting that the market will be going down.

Note: The VIX calculation uses all the out-of-the-money call and put options for the S&P 100's first and second month expirations. The goal is to estimate an implied volatility for a theoretical at-the-money option, with thirty days left until expiration.

The VIX is an optionable index. If you choose to purchase options on the VIX, you would interpret the indicators and oscillators in the same way you would for any other security's chart. On the other hand, if you want to use the VIX as an indicator to anticipate movement of the market as a whole, you will use the indicators and oscillators in reverse.

Looking at the chart above, on August 16, the highest black candle, we see that the market dropped $368 and then reversed in one day. Over the next seven weeks, the market retraced and climbed to record highs before it went through another correction.

If in reading the chart above you took notice of the crosses and oversold indicators during the week of October 8–15, you would have seen that as a good warning that the VIX was oversold, and, therefore, the market was overbought and ready for a correction. If you had been holding profit on near-term options, it would have been wise to heed its warning and sell before the drop over the next five weeks, as seen on this chart.

We can run into problems using the VIX to reflect overall sentiment for equity options, because the relationship of the VIX to individual equity options can be overstated. Volatility often is a function of market sector. For example, the technical sector is considered to be more volatile than the utility sector. Therefore, using the VIX to represent the implied volatility for all equity options tends to over simplify the big picture.

Use the VIX Index as just one more tool in our box, to be used in conjunction with others to give us the clearest picture possible of expected results.

Introducing the Greeks

The Greeks are a collection of statistical values–expressed as percentages–that give the investor a view of how the stock has been performing. These statistical values can help decide which option strategies are best to use.

The market makers use Greek designations in their calculation of option pricing–Delta, Gamma, Rho, Theta, Vega. Only two are important in checking out and choosing which option to purchase–Delta and Theta.

Delta

Delta is a theoretical value change in the option's price based on a change of the underlying's value. Specifically, this is the expected change in the option's price given a one-unit change in price of the underlying's futures contract. The range is between 0 and 1.00. This number changes as the market changes.

At optionsXpress, when you're in the process of choosing which option to purchase, you'll hold the cursor over the option symbol. A box will appear and if you scroll straight across and up to the word *Greeks,* it will display the specific Greeks for that option. This step is as important as any other information in your decision making. You want a delta that is as close to 1.00 as possible.

Let's say you decide on an option that is 0.78. This means that for every dollar that the stock price goes up, your option price will advance seventy-eight cents. If it were to be 1.00 on an option that was well up in-the-money, the option price would advance a dollar for every dollar increase in the stock's price. And that's the point that you want to achieve–for every dollar the stock moves, you also make a dollar on your option or $100 on your contract. Higher deltas come the deeper you go with in-the-money options.

What you want to avoid is the lure of an inexpensive option that is out-of-the-money. At first you think you found a great bargain–only $1.25 per contract. You imagine getting several contracts for only a few hundred dollars. But then, you check out the delta, and find it's 0.02. For every dollar move of the stock's price, you gain two cents. At this rate, it will take a long time for the option to cover the spread cost between the ask and bid price and the fees for the option transaction.

Theta

Theta represents the change in an option's value based on one-unit (7-day) changes in time, until the option is seven days out from expiration and then it changes to a one-day time frame.

This information is not used as much in the decision-making process, but is used more as you close in on your expiration date. Let's say you are forty-five days out from your expiration date. You plan to sell thirty days before that day to preserve the option's time value, but the underlying is in a period of horizontal movement. You check the theta value, which tells you the amount that your option per share is decreasing in value. If that value is 0.181, for example, that means you are losing a little more than eighteen cents a share or $18.10 on your contract per week. If your option is waffling up and down, or running horizontal, weigh the cost of your theta loss versus waiting to see what might happen over the next few days until you planned to sell anyway.

Theoretical Value

Theoretical Value is the fair market value of an option as predicted through the use of a mathematical formula. The formula takes into account the following factors–strike price, the current price of the underlying, interest rates, time remaining until expiration, dividends (if any), and implied volatility.

If you click on the underlined option symbol at an optionsXpress chain page, it brings you to information on that option. If you then scroll to the bottom of the page, you'll see on the right hand side a box with *Theoretical Data*. Click on the underlined *more information* and a page comes up that provides the theoretical value as well as the Greeks.

The theoretical value shown for each option helps to determine whether your option is fairly priced at the moment, using the current implied volatility. Theoretical value might say that the value is $1.62, but the ask price is $1.81. You would question whether the additional nineteen cents–or $19.00 on the contract of one hundred shares–is too much to pay. Perhaps the next option, the one that's deeper in-the-money is a better value, where the theoretical value is closer to the ask price.

Conversely, if the implied volatility is less than the historical volatility, the option price might seem a bargain if it is priced below its theoretical value.

Note: Those who enjoy math and calculations may find the pricing tool that runs across the top of this page useful. We can apply it when a vast difference exists between the implied volatility number and the historical volatility. Make a note of the prices of the options you are interested in, and then, in the calculator, change the implied volatility figure in the first box to that of the historical volatility. Press *calculate*. New calculations will replace the prices for the options chain on that page.

This new information shows the difference in price based on the underlying's historical volatility. Should the implied volatility drop back to its more normal range, this would be the price that you would expect to pay if you made a purchase at that time. This price difference is just one more tool to be used in your consideration.

What to Take Away for Now

This chapter covered several points, but for now, focus on and use two.

1. First, make sure the delta is as close to 1.00 as possible within your budget. Your research will illustrate that the deeper you go with in-the-money options, the higher the delta; however, the ask price will be higher, too.

2. Second, make sure that the theta's drop in value each week or day is worth the extra time you hold the option before selling.

Chapter Eleven

STRATEGIES

You've reached the end of one phase of your journey, namely the new information you need to understand and digest. You now know what you need to be a successful trader, and you have explanations of each important element, what it does, and why it is important. However, you will refer to the information again and again until you are so familiar with the indicators and chart reading that it's second nature–a routine element in your trading life.

Now it's now time to create trading strategies by using all these tools. These strategies lay out a specific strategy for success you can choose from based on your preferences. One strategy is not right for all traders.

One person's strategy might wait for the first sign or two that a stock is ready to pop, while another waits for all the indicators to be in agreement before jumping in. Based on your trading preferences and risk tolerance, one strategy or another will be more appealing.

Experiment with the different strategies in your paper and virtual trades. Find the one that you are most comfortable with. As you become more experienced, try another, until you find the one you are not only most comfortable with, but the one where you experience the most success.

Examining the Trading Strategies

Strategy #1: 7–20–50 Plus
This strategy uses the 7–20–50-day SMAs we've used throughout this book.

Calls

Use the indicators you have learned for entry and exit points.

1. Buy after a pullback, after the first close back above the 7-day SMA. A *pullback* can be a day or two of selling, or a drop-down touch or through the 20-day line or down to the 50-day. If the 50-day fails, hold and wait until it rises above the 50-day and stabilizes.

2. Cross over of 7-day SMA through 20-day and close above 7-day

3. MADC and ADX cross, preferably with low STO and rising RSI, and its positive divergence agrees with the other indicators.

Puts

Use the indicators you have learned for entry and exit points.

1. Buy after the 7-day SMA drops and crosses below and closes below the 20-day or through the 50-day.

2. MACD crosses downward and ADX cross shows –DI (red) dominating by crossing up over +DI (green) and ADX strength line (black), preferably with high STO that is dropping and the RSI heading downward and that its negative divergence agrees with the other indicators.

Strategy #2: Simple Trend, Cue, Confirmation, or STCC

Some women we've talked with asked for a bare-bones technique using a minimum number of indicators. We've devised a simple system that won't get you into a trade at the earliest moment of a new trend, but it will eliminate many of the false signals.

Calls

1. Prepare a six-month chart, using only the 40-SMA, and add only the MACD and full stochastics to the chart.

2. The first item is *trend*. We want to visibly see a rise in the 40-SMA, sloping upward. This is our *simple trend* (ST).

3. Now we need the *cue*, "C," which is the STO crossing up and over the 20 line.

4. The *confirmation*, the second "C" is a cross in the MACD shooting upward.

If the MACD cross happens below the zero line of the histogram it is still considered in *trading range.* If the cross happens above the zero line it is considered in *trending range.* Strong up-trending crosses happen above the zero line.

You will exit the trade when the MACD has reached its maximum height and flattens out. In addition, the STO will turn down and under the 80 line; or, if it flattens out, the chart will look like it is pulling back and volume will be weaker.

Puts

A put entry signal is indicated when the following occurs.

1. The *trend* signal occurs when the 40-day MA is sloping downward.

2. The *cue* is seen when the STO drops down under the 80 line.

3. The *confirmation* is a MACD cross downward.

You will exit the trade when the STO reaches twenty and the MACD reaches a low level. To use this simplified system remember to use the STCC in order.

Strategy #3

Much of the information in the IBD is geared toward investors who will actually be purchasing the underlying investments (the stocks), instead of the options covering them. However, as we've said, the information in the IBD is important for selecting option candidates, too. The IBD also advises investors with notations on their weekly charts indicating when a stock is ready to reach a point at which stock buyers should consider buying it.

If investors purchase the stock and it goes up, it means our option also goes up. So it stands to reason that if the IBD is posting buy points that investors should pay particular attention to, then we should also make note of these stocks and place their stock symbols into our chart template to evaluate their indicators.

One of the first buy points that IBD mentions is a pullback to the ten-week line (our 50-day SMA) during an extended uptrend. After a stock rebounds from a test (touch) of the 50-day SMA, it creates a new buy range for stock investors. This touch of the ten-week line acts like a trampoline and often sends the stock back up.

1. The first buy point is a few points above the 50-day line after touching that line of support.

2. The second is ten cents above the stock's previous high, coming back from a previous lazy drop of the stock or index (as opposed to a large, fast drop) while it rests before gaining a surge of energy and bounces back.

The only warning is that too many *naps* (trips to the 50-day line) may be a sign that its energy is waning and the hoped for burst is more likely to fail.

Patterns

During these periods of rest or consolidation, institutions often buy stock, which then forms a recognizable pattern that gives expected results. It's not enough that a stock breaks out of a base. That base should be a recognizable pattern.

A stock's breakout is as much a factor in the equation as the base from which it launches. You want to see the stock grab a big piece of the pie and gain volume on the day of breakout. Volume should surge to at least 50% above its average level. In general, the bigger the price and volume gain the better.

Cup and Handle Base

Its buy point is based on the resistance level of the cup's handle. In a successful pattern the handle should reflect a minor downtrend. (Upward handles are prone to failure.) A bounce up from the handle to ten cents above its highest point is the time stock buyers are advised to jump in.

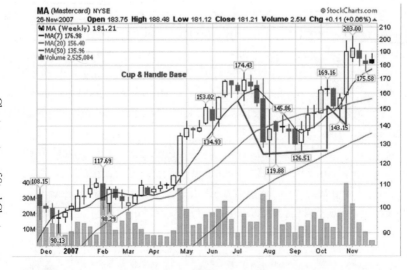

Chart courtesy of StockCharts.com

This is a weekly chart and is what the IBD uses. The buy point on MA's chart would be between $169.16 + 10 cents = $169.26 cents (the handle) and $174.43 + 10 cents = $174.53 (the high of the left side of the cup).

Other Chart Patterns

- Cup and Handle without a handle–Ten cents above the peak in left side of the base (cup)

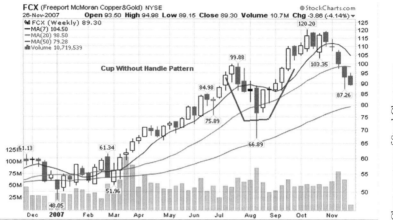

Chart courtesy of StockCharts.com

The buy point would be $99.98 on this chart.

- Cup with high handle–Ten cents above handle breakout (same as chart above) but handle near or even with high on left side that goes horizontal before jutting up in a breakout.

- Flat Base–Ten cents above the base's high

Chart courtesy of StockCharts.com

- Double Bottom–Ten cents above middle peak of the base's "W" shape.

- Three Weeks Tight–Three weeks where candles run horizontal, enter on breakout of pattern

- Four Weeks Tight–Four weeks where candles run horizontal, enter on breakout of pattern.

- Ascending Base–Enter at ten cents just above slow, steady ascent

- Late-Stage Base–Price consolidation after a leading stock has staged several breakouts from patterned bases over a long period of time.

It's usually the last base before a stock goes into a long decline. Typically, the fourth base or later ones are considered late-staged. Being watchful of these late-stage subsequent falls in price can be long-term put opportunities.

You can find a few other patterns to work with, but the ones discussed above are the ones mentioned most often in the IBD.

Note: Other advanced pattern descriptions can be found through WomenOptionsTraders.com.

Strategy #4

When a company announces and upcoming stock split, it's a strong indicator that the company is doing some things right. A stock split is exactly what it implies. A company announces that it is going to split the stock. Sometimes the split is 2-for-1. If you hold ten shares of stock, after the split you will hold twenty shares at half the present price. Other times it is 3-to-1 or 10-to-1, but the principle is the same. In a bull market, after the split, this company's stock will frequently return to a price level near the pre-split stock price.

There are several advantageous points along the stock-split-time line that are favorable for purchasing calls. Often a stock splits near the same level. We could keep a separate watch list of these stocks. Dell Computer and Microsoft are examples of this. When the price nears a historic level, we could look ahead to the next upcoming board meeting to time the purchase of our call options. Checking the information to be voted upon at the shareholders meeting will give a clue. If authorization to create new shares is on the agenda, a split could be coming.

A number of advantageous entry points to consider:

1. The first entry point would be just prior to the board meeting in anticipation of an announcement based on the proposed agenda.

2. The second entry point is at the announcement of the split, but it is hard to beat the pack. The tutes have direct, over-the-fence links. If your neighbor or brother-in-law is a broker, ask him to notify you of announcements.

3.   The third point is, if and when, within a few days of the announce-
     ment, the stock price will settle back after the initial rise. Profit-
     taking after the excitement drops the price back to its more recent
     normal level. As is often the case, the rebound will likewise be exag-
     gerated, dropping the prices lower as in a pullback. As prices begin
     to return, a long (call) position may be opened to take advantage,
     not only of the immediate rebound, but also the gradual rise as the
     stock nears the split date. Be sure that you purchase your option at
     least one month past the actual split date so as not to lose the time
     value of your option.

4.   The fourth entry point is the day or a few days prior to the split.
     Frequently, the stock will rise significantly the day of the stock split
     or in the days just before the actual split. Open the position two or
     three days before the split and then close the position toward the
     end of the last trading day prior to the actual split.

5.   The fifth entry point is in the post-split dip. About 70% of the time
     a stock will fall back in price shortly after the split. This period may
     last a day or several weeks. Put it on a watch list when you recog-
     nize the pullback, wait for the indicators to show a reversal and
     the beginning of a new trend upward, and purchase a call based on
     sound buying signals.

Some women only trade stock-splits; they go in and out of positions
on the expected dips and climbs. This strategy requires vigilant watching
of the stock's action, perhaps taking more time than some wish to devote.
However, if you're working with a computer throughout the day in some
other capacity, this may be the strategy for you.

Strategy #5: Channel Pattern Breakouts, Plus Volume

This strategy relies less on the indicators and more on the channel pattern
created by the price of the stock. It's a strategy that can be used in a flat,
up, or down market. Breakouts can signal the beginning of a long-term
new trend.

When trading channel breakouts, you look for dramatic departures from
the recent price range of a stock or an index. Wait for the price to break out
of the channel, as signaled by a daily price closing above the resistance (top)
for a call entry signal or below support (bottom) for a put entry.

Chart courtesy of StockCharts.com

The confirmation comes with a look at the volume bar for the day of the breakout. If the volume on that day is above the average recent daily volume, the trade signal is confirmed.

On occasion, there can be *false breakouts,* in that once outside the channel, price returns to that channel within a few days. To protect against loss, use support and resistance to also get you out of a trade quickly. To eliminate a large percentage of false breakouts, wait for the second day that the price closes outside the channel before entering. The downside to this strategy is that much of the breakout price move may happen before you even enter the trade.

Strategy #6: Long-term Equity AnticiPation Securities (LEAPS)

LEAPS are options that feature an extended period of time to expiration, usually as long as nine months. You can purchase a LEAPS option out a year or two. Then you only need to check the charts monthly or every few months, as you feel necessary, to verify the stock or index is on course.

Using a monthly chart can facilitate this type of trading, and you'll look primarily for the pattern created by the candlesticks. You want to select a strong IBD-rated stock that forms a pattern looking like a smile. This pattern dips on the left side and rounds at the bottom and is creating the right side of the grin. This is a positive pattern on which to invest long term. If the smile has already formed the right side, get in on the confirmed uptrend. It doesn't really matter what the stock does day-to-day or week-to-week, it will continue its upward movement of forming and breaking out of its pattern. Sell when there is some dramatic, confirmed overall market change or thirty days before the LEAPS's expiration date.

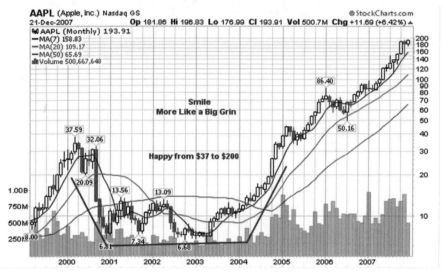

Strategy #7: Long-Range View

This strategy uses four different time periods for its entry signals, and because you are looking at a longer time frame, you would usually buy four to six months out.

1. The first signal comes from the monthly chart. It confirms the trend. You use this chart to confirm your candidate, seeing a new or strong ongoing trend.

2. The second signal comes from the weekly chart. This gives you time confirmation. You want to zero in on a week that is just beginning to trade in your direction.

3. The third signal comes from the daily chart. This gives you the entry signal when the indicators and oscillators confirm your decision.

4. The fourth signal comes from the 60-minute chart. This gives you the buy signal, the specific minute to push the buy button. You stalk this trade, waiting for the indicator crosses in your direction.

What to Watch for Once You Are in a Trade

Once you have purchased an option, you will watch the chart to gauge how it is doing. In order to understand what might happen next in its movement, it is important to remember the saying: *price has memory.* What we mean by this is to watch areas of support and resistance, beyond the ceiling and floors that we have already discussed. Other areas of resistance and support might be more like landings between floor levels. In the past, we can see areas on a chart where either a great deal of buying or selling has taken place. These plateaus are mini-blockades that stall or prevent forward movement. Often they create mirror images on a chart, where the right side creates a pattern quite like the pattern on the left.

This chart shows several areas of resistance and also some recognizable patterns.

- #1–This is the left shoulder in a head and shoulder pattern. These are a series of rolling pumps that can be visualized as a left shoulder, head, and then right shoulder. There are times when reading a chart you can anticipate that this formation is in the making, thus giving you a clue as to the next direction the chart will take. We may also see the reverse of this pattern—an inverted head and shoulders pattern, resembling a person standing on her head.

- #2—This is the head in this head and shoulder pattern.

- #3—This is the right shoulder in the pattern. The left shoulder, which you can see only a portion of on this chart, created buy resistance on the left side of the chart. The right side stalled at this place of resistance and couldn't rise any further. This area of resistance is created by the buyers who purchased stock back in June, who didn't sell when it reached the high price at the head; they've waited for it to reach their buy point again, so they can sell their stock without taking a loss. That selling creates the drop in price that creates the right shoulder.

- #4—This is a double bottom pattern mention earlier. Here support seems to be in the $125 range, which won't allow the stock to drop beyond that point.

- #5—Here we stall for a few days as it reached the point of resistance on the left side of the chart created by both the left and right shoulder. We repeat, price has memory. A couple of days' drop in price shakes out any one who bought and is still holding since early August.

- # 6—We see more resistance created by the right shoulder's high price. It is waiting for extra volume to move beyond that former high level between the right shoulder and the head.

- #7—This shows resistance created by buying at the high price, the point of the head. We see the effort over at least ten days to break out to a new high.

- #8—Failing to break out, we see the stock pull back to rest and regain its strength. It tried again on November 19, but failed to hold itself above that level. It dropped again, creating a double bottom, which is a bullish pattern. We might think that on this last leg of the W it will be successful and will breakout to new highs. Seeing this double bottom pattern, we would consider purchasing a call option on ICE once the last candlestick closes above the 7-day SMA or as signaled by other indicators.

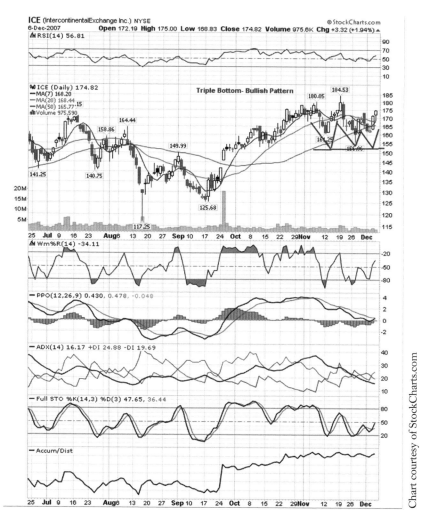

As an example, we've included a more recent chart on ICE to check the development of the W pattern. Rather than fully completing the double bottom pattern and then rising to new highs, the stock dropped back in price and formed a triple bottom (bullish) pattern. Notice on the chart above that the indicators (PPO and ADX) never crossed on the second leg up, but are about to do so now.

Also, if you run your eye along the price area between $155 and $165, notice all the candles that come to rest at that point, either stopping and not dropping further or stopping and not rising high. This is further example of the support and resistance at that price point, further stressing that price has memory.

Let's take another look three weeks later.

Chart courtesy of StockCharts.com

On December 10, ICE retraced, coming close to its old high near $180. For another three days, it hung out, testing that area of resistance, until it finally built the strength to break through that line on December 14. It then climbed, forming a new uptrend with plenty of tute support, seen in the high, level A/D line.

Recognizing patterns and spotting areas of support and resistance helps to interpret what might take place over the coming days and weeks, giving you an indication of what to expect and how long it might take to move beyond the obstacles. Using this information in conjunction with your expiration date helps to zero in and pinpoint sell signals.

Other Useful Information

They say a picture is worth a thousand words, and the same can be said for chart reading. If we remove all the indicators–RSI, MACD, STO, Williams

%R, A/D, and volume–we are left with the candlestick. As explained earlier, the top of the candlestick displays the daily or weekly high, while the bottom provides the lows.

The location of where on the candlestick the close happens helps us gauge whether institutional investors–who account for at least 75% of a leading stock's action–are involved and lending support. It's a good sign that the pack is involved if the candlestick closes in the upper half of its daily or weekly range. That means the crazed wolves are snapping up shares, prompting prices to rise or at least to hold firm.

A stock that often closes near its session lows signals that the pack maybe heading out the back door and selling. It can still be an up day (hollow candle), but the cross happens in the bottom half of the body of the candle. This signals that though it was an up day, there was a lot of selling taking place.

The close of the trading session becomes even more important as a stock forms a base pattern. You want to see a stock in the upper half of its daily or weekly range at the bottom of its base. A bullish reversal at the bottom of the base is also a positive sign. That happens when a stock drops sharply but ends up recouping most, if not all, of its loss. In such a case the close should be very near the top of the candlestick.

You also want to see a stock or Index close near the top of its range as it builds the right side of a base and as it hits new highs.

Go back to the last few charts that we included to show patterns. Notice where the candles closed as the bottom of the base pattern was being formed. Where did the candles close as they formed the right side of the pattern? How did they look on the breakout? The more you study the charts, the more you'll see the patterns.

When to Start, When to Wait

The principles you've learned here are most effective in the *trending market* (steady long-term movement up or down). A *trading market* is a bit more erratic and advanced and requires more everyday attention to the market. In other words, it's a trickier environment for beginners. So, those new to trading should stand aside under trading conditions until they have garnered more experience.

In the trending market, we see relatively major increases in price over a longer period of time (shorter times for declines and corrections). This market condition occurs a couple of times a year during most years. Within trading markets, you'll see alternating smaller cycles of up and down movement, usually within a channel. Otherwise, trading markets with lots of whipsaws—up and down prices—can alternate in that cycle.

Allow the indicators to tell you when it is time to buy or sell. You are the one who has to live with your trading decisions. Do not allow fear, greed, or impatience to manage your trading.

The wise trader knows how to manage her money well. She knows the buy and sell signals and doesn't take unnecessary risks. It is a good idea to limit your losses to a certain percentage (15%–20%) of your initial investment, and this is tempered by the expiration date. If you reach a loss point at the level you set, or the more generalized 50% loss sell rule, get out and wait for a better day.

If you don't purchase the chart listing service offered by StockCharts. com, giving you the tools to maintain a list of candidates, remember we offer a list of charts of IBD top-rated stocks and indexes at our Internet site, www.WomenOptionTraders.com.

Trading should be relaxed and fun, colored by confident, positive expectations; we don't believe trading should ever be stressful. In fact, we believe you should never trade when you are feeling stressed.

Stick to your money management plan. Keep your emotions in check, follow your trading rules and strategies, and you'll be a successful trader.

Chapter Twelve

WORKING THE PLAN

At last, you've reached the stage in which you'll develop your *system*. By now you realize that you'll never simply say, "I guess I'll buy an option contract on Apple today." That way of thinking isn't a system at all–and it almost certainly leads to loss and disappointment. But since your trading system or methodology has well-defined rules of entry and exit, plus rules for choosing whose stock and which option contract to purchase, you'll not be making haphazard choices.

By its nature, a system has a firm, even rigid set of rules and measurements. The hardest thing about a trading system is following the rules. As we've said, emotions tend to get in the way. It bears repeating: *form and apply good trading habits.*

Okay, so far, you've taken to studying the *Investor's Business Daily* and making a list of investment candidates, recording them in a notebook dedicated just to trading issues. You've also created a few headings across the top of the pages. Eventually, as you move along, you'll have two hundred to three hundred stock candidates to choose from.

Security Symbol	Price	EPS	Rel	Str	Grp	Str	Notes
	($25–50+)		80+		90+		(A-B)

Because we were able to pick up so many on our first few cruises through the newspaper, we may have quite a few in alphabetical order, such as AA, APPL, ABFS, AKS, APA, BA.

The next step is to create your own charts, becoming familiar with the chart variations available to you. The Internet site we've found most useful in creating clear, understandable charts is www.StockCharts.com. Most of the charts you've seen in this book were created on that site.

StockCharts.com offers free charting services. In addition, at some future point, if you decide it would be advantageous to keep a list of charts to view at any given moment, StockCharts.com offers that service as well. (At the time this book went to print, we could save and view up to five hundred lists with five hundred charts each for under $20.) This isn't absolutely necessary, but it's quite handy.

This company offers other services, such as real time price movement on the charts, rather than fifteen-minute delays. This service is an additional $10. However, real time is available at no cost at the sites where option purchases are made, so as a beginning option trader, we don't recommend this expense, at least until you become crazy about trading like many of us have.

We are aware of a few other charting services. MoneyCentral.MSN. com/investors/charts, BigCharts.com, and Profitspi.com offer free charts, but we don't have any direct experience using them. A number of sites offer charting software available to download at a cost.

However, based on our experience, we've found StockCharts.com effective and versatile. We also post and maintain a list of highly-rated IBD stock charts, under Public Charts on their site, and then, as you scroll down you'll find, *Women Option Traders'* public charts.

Once you go to StockCharts.com, click on the *Free Charts* tab in the middle-right. In the square titled *Sharp Charts,* type the symbol of your first candidate.

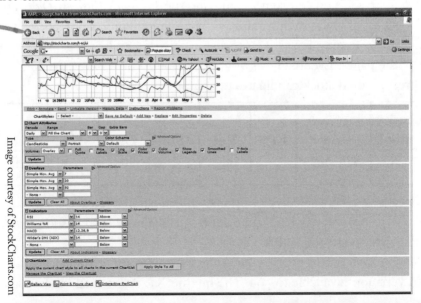

Image courtesy of StockCharts.com

You'll see on the image of the chart above, that *chart styles* and *indicators* can be changed to your preferences. We like the portrait-sized chart, instead of the default 460. The *Overlays* has drop-down boxes, so that you can add and change the *Simple Moving Averages* to those of seven-days, twenty-days, and fifty-days. At some future point you may want to check out some other time reference. That option is open to you.

Periods and *Range* allow you to set a time frame; most often we leave it at "Fill the chart," which gives an optimum view of information.

Further down the page you'll see *Indicators,* which also has drop-down boxes. The free charting allows you to choose three or four indicators. If and when you decide to become a StockCharts.com member, the number of indicators is unlimited, but using more than a half dozen can be too complicated.

Once you set the parameters that you want to use, click *Update.* Anytime you change a symbol, or make an indicator or size change, you'll need to click *Update.* This charting template can be bookmarked or saved to your favorites on your computer.

You can also click the *Print* option at the bottom of the chart if you would like a hard copy of a chart to study or to preserve as a reference that shows why you chose a particular option to get into.

After you feel comfortable with the chart making process, play around, and check out the different time periods. Look at a chart over three months, six months, one year, and two years. All this gives a whole new perspective on what has occurred in the past with a particular company.

Now that you have your chart setup, you can delete the symbol in the upper left corner of the chart, add another candidate, click update, and view that company's information. Review each candidate as we have discussed, applying the indicators.

In your notebook, write today's date on a page and as you find a candidate that looks ripe, write its symbol down and maybe a few reference notes. If a candidate doesn't look like it is ready today, but is worth watching and you think it might be prime in two days, place the dates of the next two days on subsequent pages and write the symbol under the date you want to be reminded to check that chart again.

Go through your list as you have time, sizing up the charts. You'll find that some are not of interest, but others draw your attention immediately. Once you have a few listed under today's date, you can go back and review them, narrowing down the candidates to only those with the greatest potential.

- Is there one that seems more stable, reliable in nature, and less volatile?

- Is there one that seems to move in larger dollar increments?

- Is there one where all or most of the indicators agree?

- Has the price either just pulled back and then had another day to come back up? Or has a day just closed over the 7-day SMA after a downward movement?

- Review the buy signals.

Before we discuss which option on a super-stock-candidate we choose to purchase from the option chain, let's look at two more charts. Thus far we have looked only at daily charts, although we've mentioned the importance of checking out the weekly chart to get a look at the bigger picture.

Next to the box in the upper left where you placed the symbol of your candidates, there is a drop down box that says *Periods.* Click *Weekly,* and

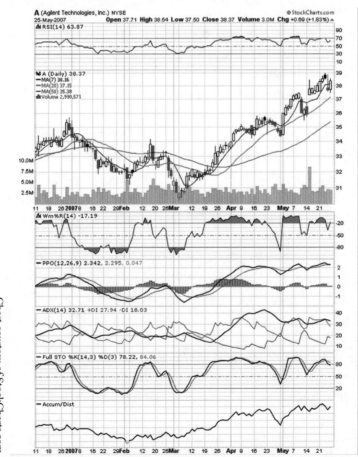

Chart courtesy of StockCharts.com

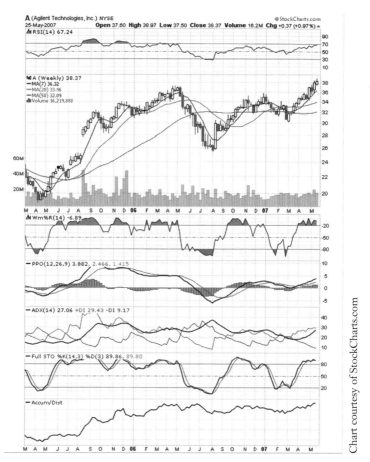

then *Update.* The next two charts listed below are daily and weekly charts on the same company, covering the same period of time.

Let's analyze these charts.

Each of the candlesticks on the weekly chart includes its corresponding five days from the daily chart. The last five candles' price movement on the daily chart are incorporated in the size and amount in the last candle on the weekly chart. Four days up and one big price movement down netted a week's change of +.37 cents. If it is Tuesday, the last weekly candle includes only the first two days of that week.

You can apply the indicators you've learned to read in the same manner to the weekly chart, confirming up-trends and downward movement. Notice on this weekly chart how clearly you can see an upward trend since March. This broader picture can help confirm either a decision to buy or sell. At this point in time, this weekly chart shows strong upward trend momentum. Also, notice the squeeze that initiated at least four months of upward movement, taking the price from $26 to $34.

The put purchase opportunity in May of 2006 ran until August of that year.

Other Tools

Once you have found a few candidates, it is advisable to see when they report their company earnings. The information can be found at www.Earnings.com. The home page lists the companies that will be reporting earnings on the current day. In the upper right-hand corner, you'll see a box to type the symbol you are interested in. Click *Go* and it will bring up the company's page. Sometimes the earnings report date is listed at the top of the page under *Events*. Other times you'll need to skim down the page to *Earnings Releases* to find the information you need.

You will also find other interesting information listed here. For example, you can check to see if the earnings reported in the last few quarterly reports met or beat the estimates. As we've said, holding an option up to or over a reporting date can be tricky. Often a company has had pre-earnings run up before the reporting date, and then, even with great earnings, the stock drops. At other times, it will run horizontal for a week or two, waiting for the news and will breakout if its earnings and outlook are good, or it will drop through and violate support if the news is poor.

You may also find www.finance.yahoo.com a useful tool. When the page comes up, you'll see a spot at the top where you can type in your symbol, then click *Symbol Lookup*. Again, type in your symbol on the next page that appears, and on the following page, click on the underlined symbol that matches your company. The new page that appears shows the day's stock activity, prices, movement, and a small chart; it also lists news headlines that relate to this company.

This free site also lets you look up past news articles. If you are wondering why a stock dropped six months ago, you can go back to that date in order to look it up and find out. By the way, this site has a membership program for a fee. However, we're familiar only with the free service.

Once you set up an option trading account with any of the online trading companies you'll have access to these news articles. However, in many ways, this Yahoo site is a convenient way to retrieve pertinent information.

BigCharts.com is also a convenient site on which to size up option chains. Once you believe you're ready to open a trading account (to open an account you don't need to fund it—no money is required.), the chains will be available there, using real time information. BigCharts.com offers easy charts to read, though their information is delayed by fifteen minutes. This site is great for paper trading before you step into virtual trading or using the real money you've put into your account. You can also obtain option chain information through the Chicago Board of Options Exchange (CBOE) at www.CBOE.com. BigCharts.com also offers charting services, but over time, we found StockCharts.com preferable. However, you might make a different choice after you have experience with each.

Option Chain Chart

Earlier, we briefly discussed the option chain chart, but now we will look at it more closely, and then we'll select an option candidate and go through the steps of the so-called paper trading that we've referred to throughout the book.

To get to the chain at BigCharts.com, insert the symbol in the box at the top of the page and click *Basic Charts.* The page that comes up will show a

Symbol	Last	Change	Vol	Bid	Ask	Open Int.	StrikePrice	Symbol	Last	Change	Vol	Bid	Ask	Open Int.
CATFN	5.91	+0.21	17.00	6.00	6.10	1,545.00	70.00	CATRN	0.20	-0.06	133.00	0.18	0.20	3,189.00
CATFA	3.65	+0.05	232.00	3.75	3.85	3,788.00	72.50	CATRA	0.45	-0.13	102.00	0.45	0.45	4,508.00
CATFO	1.95	+0.05	837.00	1.95	1.98	7,062.00	75.00	CATRO	1.12	-0.16	624.00	1.08	1.12	5,128.00

Stock Price ▶ 75.71 Last as of 6/26/2007

Symbol	Last	Change	Vol	Bid	Ask	Open Int.	StrikePrice	Symbol	Last	Change	Vol	Bid	Ask	Open Int.
CATFP	0.23	-0.04	279.00	0.24	0.27	6,458.00	80.00	CATRP	4.55	-0.20	24.00	4.40	4.50	1,254.00
CATFQ	0.04	-0.01	197.00	0.02	0.04	2,199.00	85.00	CATRQ	9.50	+1.62	44.00	9.25	9.55	2.00

Hide July, 2007 Options

Symbol	Last	Change	Vol	Bid	Ask	Open Int.	StrikePrice	Symbol	Last	Change	Vol	Bid	Ask	Open Int.
CATGL	17.50	+0.10	11.00	15.95	16.30	11.00	60.00	CATSL	0.11		25.00	0.11	0.13	
CATGM	11.25	-1.45	57.00	11.35	11.50	113.00	65.00	CATSM	0.32	-0.03	45.00	0.29	0.32	23.00
CATGU	9.00	-0.05	23.00	9.10	9.20	105.00	67.50	CATSU	0.55	-0.06	15.00	0.51	0.54	42.00
CATGN	6.90	+0.20	271.00	6.95	7.05	266.00	70.00	CATSN	0.93	-0.08	26.00	0.87	0.91	1,109.00
CATGA	4.96	-0.13	457.00	5.00	5.10	375.00	72.50	CATSA	1.55	-0.10	49.00	1.47	1.50	832.00
CATGO	3.35		230.00	3.40	3.50	1,518.00	75.00	CATSO	2.52	-0.14	169.00	2.37	2.42	1,308.00

Stock Price ▶ 75.71 Last as of 6/26/2007

Symbol	Last	Change	Vol	Bid	Ask	Open Int.	StrikePrice	Symbol	Last	Change	Vol	Bid	Ask	Open Int.
CATGP	1.27		186.00	1.28	1.30	2,192.00	80.00	CATSP	5.05	-0.60	160.00	5.25	5.35	502.00
CATGQ	0.41	-0.01	10.00	0.37	0.40	509.00	85.00	CATSQ	9.25	-0.35	55.00	9.40	9.50	45.00
CATGR	0.11	-0.05	1.00	0.09	0.12	21.00	90.00	CATSR	13.85			31.00	14.25	14.60
CATGS				0.02	0.05		95.00	CATSS	18.85			20.00	19.25	19.55

Hide August, 2007 Options

Symbol	Last	Change	Vol	Bid	Ask	Open Int.	StrikePrice	Symbol	Last	Change	Vol	Bid	Ask	Open Int.
CATHW	26.15	-0.30	13.00	28.25	28.65	243.00	47.50	CATTW	0.03	-0.01	8.00	0.03	0.05	1,432.00
CATHJ	25.00	-1.65	1.00	25.85	26.15	337.00	50.00	CATTJ	0.11	+0.01	10.00	0.04	0.08	8,233.00
CATHX	23.50	-1.30	10.00	23.40	23.70	344.00	52.50	CATTX	0.10	-0.05	10.00	0.08	0.10	6,080.00
CATHK	22.35	+1.40	30.00	20.95	21.25	633.00	55.00	CATTK	0.15	-0.01	40.00	0.12	0.15	26,336.00
CATHY	18.70	+0.85	40.00	18.50	18.85	398.00	57.50	CATTY	0.20	-0.05	41.00	0.18	0.20	3,234.00
CATHL	15.90	-0.85	15.00	16.10	16.45	1,557.00	60.00	CATTL	0.30	+0.04	4.00	0.26	0.28	14,583.00
CATHZ	15.20	+1.25	49.00	13.80	14.10	1,401.00	62.50	CATTZ	0.43	+0.08	8.00	0.38	0.41	2,657.00
CATHM	11.50		6.00	11.65	11.80	5,884.00	65.00	CATTM	0.63	+0.08	3.00	0.57	0.60	6,531.00
CATHU	9.45	-0.05	15.00	9.45	9.60	6,799.00	67.50	CATTU	0.89	-0.11	228.00	0.86	0.90	3,623.00
CATHN	7.36	-0.14	122.00	7.45	7.55	4,899.00	70.00	CATTN	1.39	-0.09	252.00	1.30	1.35	2,414.00
CATHA	5.55	+0.05	13.00	5.60	5.70	2,059.00	72.50	CATTA	2.00	-0.13	36.00	1.97	2.01	4,437.00
CATHO	4.00		164.00	4.05	4.10	8,358.00	75.00	CATTO	2.97	-0.18	136.00	2.88	2.94	1,858.00

Stock Price ▶ 75.71 Last as of 6/26/2007

Symbol	Last	Change	Vol	Bid	Ask	Open Int.	StrikePrice	Symbol	Last	Change	Vol	Bid	Ask	Open Int.
CATHP	1.83	+0.02	69.00	1.83	1.86	6,462.00	80.00	CATTP	5.70	+0.25	423.00	5.60	5.75	641.00
CATHQ	0.75	-0.08	8.00	0.68	0.71	3,509.00	85.00	CATTQ	9.75	+1.10	21.00	9.55	9.65	972.00

basic chart of your company or index. Above the chart in the middle of the page you'll see an underlined heading *Options chain;* click it, and the chain for that stock or index will come up.

We've opened this option chain for Caterpillar (CAT) to show June, July, and August options. You can click *Hide June, 2007 Options* if you are not interested in those and open others further out in time if you choose. Although BigCharts.com does not always show all the months for which options are available, brokerage firms do show them all. But, to learn to read a chain and for paper trading, the information BigCharts.com shows works just fine.

As we have noted before, the calls are on the left and puts are on the right. The dark cell that runs through the center with $75.71 is the current market price for CAT's stock. The strike prices of the options available appear above and below the market price.

If there was a strike price listed for $75.71, it would be *in-the-money.* Options in the darker shaded areas at the upper left and lower right of each month are all in-the-money. The options in the lighter shaded areas at the upper right and lower left corner of each month are *out-of-the-money.*

Take a look at the price differences as the intrinsic value or lack of it is reflected as you move either deeper in-the-money or further out-of-the-money. Note the difference in price, for example, of a $75 June option at $1.98, the $75 July option at $3.50, and the August $75 at $4.10. The June option has about twenty days until expiration. We must question whether we believe our stock position will develop in the course of those twenty days, or (as we advise) should a July or August option be purchased, giving us either an additional thirty or sixty days time for our position to show a profit. (Remember, options expire on the third Friday of the expiration month.)

You will recall that each option has a different symbol and an option is on a block of one hundred shares of stock. The $75 strike price options above would cost $198, $350, or $410, depending on which expiration month you chose.

The column marked *last* reflects the last price paid for the option before it moved to its present ask price. Notice the *bid* and *ask prices.* The difference between these two prices is a fee paid to the market makers who setup the options. You will always pay the higher of these two when you buy, and receive the lower of these two when you sell.

If we bought the July $75 option, we would pay $350 (this amount is taken out of our account), and if we turned around the next minute and sold it, we would receive $340 (this amount would be added to our account). The $10 difference is the market maker's fee. The fee varies on the price of the underlying stock and volatility. We discuss volatility in an earlier chapter.

Volume (Vol) and *open interest* (Open Int) reflect the amount of activity surrounding the particular option. We generally say we should jump on an option that the pack has jumped on first, so unless there is a fair amount of volume, use extreme caution. Our rule is one hundred or more in volume.

Note on the chart above that there was good interest in the June $75 option; those traders may have purchased earlier in April and May. There is less interest in July, and an even greater number in August. These numbers indicate that the pack is more interested in the August option, but we can pick up information beyond that. For example, maybe Caterpillar is a cyclical stock that shows more profits more during the summer months when more building, grading, or earth-moving services are performed. Maybe the stock has consolidated and is coming out of a pattern that looks like it will take a month to breakout. This information would be seen on their chart, either in a current pattern or cyclical information could be determined by looking back on their chart to this time last year. You would then want to give your option plenty of time for this pattern to develop, giving additional time for unexpected delays.

When you begin trading, paper or virtual, it is wise to give yourself two to three months margin of time. This means you choose an expiration date that is two to three months in the future, allowing plenty of time for the security to go up. This reduces worry and is a form of insurance, because you don't have to hold an option out to the full term of its expiration.

Don't get tripped up with a thought that goes something like this: "But I paid extra to buy out in time those two months, so I think I should hold on another few weeks." *If you have made a nice profit, and the chart says a change is about to happen, don't hang on thinking that you can*

Wise Option Traders Remember
Four times a year futures, options on stocks, and options on indexes expire on the same day. This is called triple witching, *and usually results in higher volatility and volume.*

weather whatever the change might bring and come out making more on the other side. Take your profit. You'll have your investment money plus your profit, and you can purchase another hot option, rather than tie your money and yourself into a knot while you wait for the situation to improve and reach its former height. How much more could have been made during that time with an option that was ready to breakout or move up quickly?

Let's say that back on May 1, we made a paper trade purchase on Ceradyne (CRDN). We purchased option AUEIK 55 Sept, after the stock had pulled back and again started to move up. We paid $7.25 per share or a total of $725.

The chart is pictured below, along with the current option chain to show our profit if we decide to sell the option today, since the stock dropped for three days, even though we still have four months left. With this amount of time remaining on our option, in actuality based on the chart below, we very well might not choose to sell since some of the

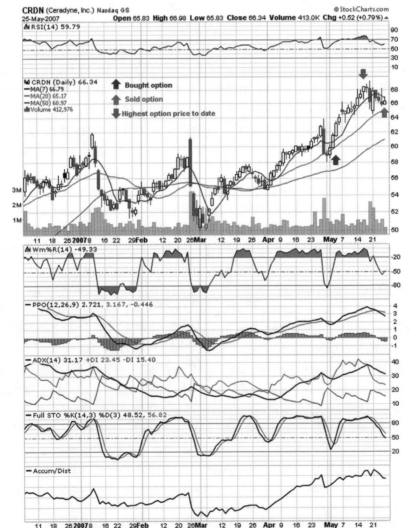

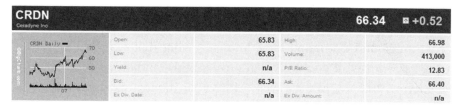

| CRDN Ceradyne Inc | | | | | | | 66.34 | +0.52 |
| | | | | | | | | |

Open:	65.83	High:	66.98
Low:	65.83	Volume:	413,000
Yield:	n/a	P/E Ratio:	12.83
Bid:	66.34	Ask:	66.40
Ex Div. Date:	n/a	Ex Div. Amount:	n/a

E✶TRADE   Get 100 commission-free trades   E*TRADE Securities

OPTION CHAIN FOR CERADYNE INC

	CALLS							PUTS					
Symbol	Last	Change	Vol	Bid	Ask	Open Int.	StrikePrice	Symbol	Last	Change	Vol	Bid	Ask	Open Int.
AUEIG	30.70	+4.20	10.00	31.70	32.20	40.00	35.00	AUEUG	0.70	-0.10	175.00	0.05	0.10	99.00
AUEIH	22.30	+2.30	10.00	26.90	27.30	53.00	40.00	AUEUH	0.18	-0.12	10.00	0.10	0.20	192.00
AUEII	22.20	+1.10	2.00	22.20	22.60	27.00	45.00	AUEUI	0.40	-0.05	3.00	0.30	0.40	558.00
AUEIJ	18.02	+0.62	10.00	17.70	18.10	162.00	50.00	AUEUJ	0.75	-0.15	5.00	0.70	0.80	628.00
AUEIK	13.72	-1.38	10.00	13.50	13.80	348.00	55.00	AUEUK	1.44	-0.06	34.00	1.40	1.55	696.00
AUEIL	10.20	-0.10	1.00	9.80	10.00	652.00	60.00	AUEUL	2.55	-0.20	25.00	2.50	2.70	1,319.00
AUEIM	6.40	-0.10	4.00	6.50	6.80	1,013.00	65.00	AUEUM	4.20	+0.10	6.00	4.20	4.40	998.00
						Stock Price ▶	66.34	Last as of 5/25/2007					
AUEIN	4.20	+0.20	36.00	4.10	4.20	1,500.00	70.00	AUEUN	8.20	+0.90	30.00	6.60	6.90	153.00
AUEIO	2.80	+0.35	2.00	2.20	2.35	765.00	75.00	AUEUO	10.00	+0.50	4.00	9.90	10.10	14.00
AUEIP	1.40	-0.10	7.00	1.05	1.20	185.00	80.00	AUEUP	21.80	+2.40	18.00	13.90	14.20	

Show June, 2007 Options
Show July, 2007 Options
Hide September, 2007 Options
Show December, 2007 Options
Show January, 2008 Options
Show January, 2009 Options

indicators appear to be showing that the price might rise again. However, we wanted to show the profit made in twenty-five days, since the chart gave the sell signal of a candle's close below the 7-day SMA.

Several sell signals happened around May 20, but the current stock price is close to what it would have been on that day. Therefore, the value of the option is also close to that day's price.

Option AUEIK would sell for $13.50. If sold today, deducting the $7.25 we paid for the contract, our profit is $6.25 per share or $625, made in the twenty-five days since we purchased the contract. The highest price the option reached was $14.98 when the stock was at $68.20 on the chart before it dropped $2.

Paper trading is a great way to begin the process of option trading. It will help you build confidence in how you are evaluating the charts and selecting companies. Go through your candidates to find ones that look as if they are bound to go up, based on their charts. Go to BigCharts.com and look at the options chain. Check out the costs for different months with the same strike price nearest in-the-money. Give yourself an allotted amount to invest in your paper trading account. Will you start with $500? $1,000? $2,000?

Check out the latest news on the company you select. When is its next earnings report due out? Once you have settled on a company and option strike price and expiration date, knowing what that option selection will cost, ask yourself if you are willing to risk this amount; at the same time, you know that you can sell well before your money dissipates if the stock changes course.

You know when to sell based on the indicators on the chart. If you decide to purchase the option, note the details on a page in your notebook. Note down the loss at which you would sell–the 7% rule–if it changed directions immediately. As your option advances, calculate a mental figure indicating when you will sell if it starts to drop, while you have a great deal of time left. Otherwise follow the thirty-day sell rule. When you do sell the contract, write down the details,

Date	Name	Quantity	Buy to Open Symbol	Sell to Close	Price	Expiration	Total	Net
5/1/07	Ceradyne	1	.AUEIK-Call		$7.25	Sept	$725.00	
5/25/07		1		.AUEIK	$13.50	Sept	$1350.00	$625.00

The Cost of Trading

We haven't yet talked about trading fees. However, as you know, brokers charge a fee to handle trades, both buying and selling options, usually about $15 each way. However, that fee is sometimes lowered if an investor makes a large number of trades over a period of three months. So, when we calculate our profits, we must deduct the transaction fee. In the example above, we would deduct an additional $30 from the $625, showing a net profit of $595. Of course, you can also view it from the *rate of return* point of view. Our $595 profit is an 82% return on our investment, made over the period of twenty-five days!

So, practice! Invest, and invest some more. Gain experience on paper, just as if it were with real money–all the principles, the companies, and process are exactly the same.

Chapter Thirteen

THE PATTERN FUNNEL NARROWS

Thus far, we've discussed major patterns that stocks and indexes create as they move through their annual growth periods viewed from the broader portion of our forecasting funnel, such as cups and handles, double bottoms, and so forth, which provide entry signals. Now we'll look at bullish and bearish patterns that can be created over shorter time periods and that often signal which direction the security may be heading in next. Then, as we observe the correlation of one candlestick to the candlesticks on either side of it and examine the pattern they create, we'll follow the security's price flow down and out of the funnel.

We've grouped the patterns into bullish, bearish, and continuation or neutral pattern categories.

The Patterns–Triangles, Wedges, Flags, and Pennants

Wedge patterns are formed by two lines, each of which points in the same direction–up, down, or horizontal. The triangular shape appears as a wedge. Wedges are, in our opinion, some of the most reliable chart patterns for predicting future price movement.

Bullish Patterns–Falling Wedges

A descending or falling wedge's triangular shape is created by two boundary lines moving downward with the higher line having the steepest angle of descent. This pattern will normally break upward because the steepest angle

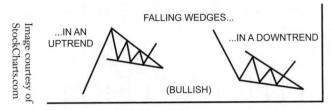

of ascent is the least sustainable. As the candlesticks descend into the ever-narrowing apex of the wedge, the price usually breaks up and out, either continuing the upward trend or, in the case of a downtrend, reverses its downward movement, creating a new leg up.

Bullish Pennant

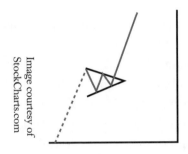

Typically, *pennants* are formed by a price spike, perhaps in connection with the introduction of a new product or favorable earnings report. This spike in price forms the mast or flagpole of the pennant. The flag portion typically runs horizontal rather than rising or dropping downward. It is similar in appearance to what is known in stock market jargon as a *continuation symmetrical triangle* or *wedge* but covers a shorter duration of time. The pattern is a pause in the uptrend, reflected by a decrease in volume. A spike in volume indicates a breakout, resuming the uptrend.

Bullish Flag

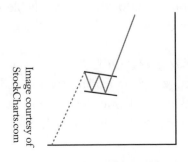

A *bullish flag pattern* is similar in formation to the bullish pennant. The difference is that resistance and support lines run parallel creating a rectangular flag, rather than converging to create a pointed pennant. The pattern is the product of price consolidation.

The vertical uptrend that precedes a flag may occur as a reaction to a favorable earnings report or new product launch. The sharp price increase is sometimes referred to as the flagpole or mast.

When speaking about flags, analysts often use jargon referring to the flag as *flying at half mast*. This term refers to the pattern being at a midpoint of what would otherwise be a continuous uptrend.

This pattern can take as few as five days to form, but usually takes no longer than two weeks and should form on lower volume. When it breaks out, it should happen on increased volume.

Megaphone Bottom

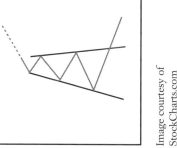

Image courtesy of StockCharts.com

A *megaphone bottom pattern*, also known as a broadening bottom, is a rare pattern, indicating that the current downtrend may reverse to form a new uptrend. It is the opposite of the bullish symmetrical triangle.

The pattern develops after a strong downtrend. The pattern can last several weeks or even a few months before completion. A megaphone bottom is formed because the security makes a series of higher highs and lower lows, usually consisting of two ascending peaks between three descending troughs. The signal that the pattern is complete is when the price rises above the line or the highest high.

Double Bottom

We discussed the double bottom pattern and the triple bottom during our review of charts; we won't repeat the information, but we list it here to clarify its inclusion with other bullish patterns.

Triple Bottom

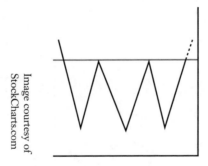

A *triple bottom* can be considered a variation of the head and shoulders pattern that we discussed in an earlier chapter. The main difference is that the bottom-most peaks of the triple bottom are more or less at the same level, where the head and shoulder displays a higher peak in the middle, the head, between the two shoulders. The triple bottom signals a downtrend is in the process of becoming an uptrend.

Head & Shoulders–Bottom

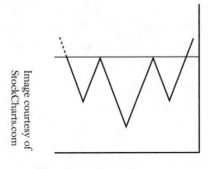

Bearish Patterns–Rising Wedges

Ascending or *rising wedges* are created by two boundary lines moving upward, with the lower line having the steepest angle of ascent. This pattern will normally break downward because the steepest angle of ascent is the least sustainable. As the candlesticks ascend into the ever-narrowing apex of the wedge, the price usually breaks down and out, either continuing the downtrend or, in the case of an uptrend, reverses it upward movement, creating a new leg down.

Bearish Pennant

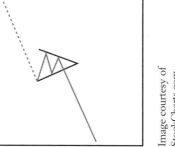

Pennants are typically formed by a price spike, perhaps in connection with negative news or an unfavorable earnings report. This drop in price forms the mast or flagpole of the pennant. The flag portion typically runs horizontal rather than rising or dropping downward. It is similar in appearance to a symmetrical continuation triangle or wedge but covers a shorter duration of time. The pattern is a pause in the downtrend, reflected by a decrease in volume. A spike in volume indicates a breakout, resuming the downtrend.

Bearish Flag

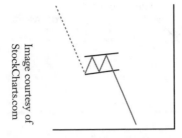

Image courtesy of StockCharts.com

A *bearish flag pattern* is similar in formation to the bearish pennant. The difference is that resistance and support lines run parallel, creating a rectangle flag, rather than converging to create a pointed pennant. The pattern is the product of price consolidation.

The vertical downtrend, which precedes a flag, may occur as a reaction to an unfavorable earnings report or negative news. As explained above, the sharp price decrease is sometimes referred to as the flagpole or mast.

This pattern can take as few as five days to form but usually takes no longer than two weeks to complete the pattern and should form on lower volume. When it breaks out it should happen on increased volume.

Megaphone Top Pattern

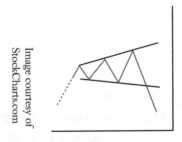

Image courtesy of StockCharts.com

A *megaphone top pattern* also known as a *broadening top* is a rare pattern, indicating that the current uptrend may reverse to form a new downtrend. It is the opposite of the bearish symmetrical triangle.

The pattern develops after a strong uptrend. The pattern can last several weeks or even a few months before completion. A megaphone top is formed because the security makes a series of higher highs and lower lows, usually consisting of three ascending peaks and two descending troughs. The signal that the pattern is complete is when the price falls below the line or the lowest low.

Double Top

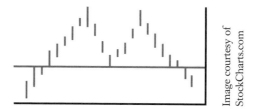

Image courtesy of StockCharts.com

A *double top* occurs when price candlesticks form two distinct peaks. A double top is complete when prices decline below the lowest low of the valley floor or the middle trough of the M. The double top is a reversal pattern of an uptrend and signals that an uptrend is in the process of becoming a downtrend. It is one of the most frequently seen patterns and because it is so easy to identify, the double top should be a signal to approach an option with caution.

Triple Top

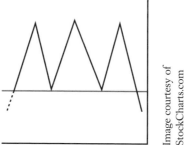

Image courtesy of StockCharts.com

A *triple top* can be considered a variation of the head and shoulders pattern that we discussed in an earlier chapter. The main difference is that the topmost peaks of the triple top are more or less at the same level, where the head and shoulder displays a higher peak in the middle, the head, between the two shoulders.

The triple top signals and uptrend is in the process of becoming a downtrend.

Head and Shoulders–Top

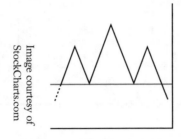

The *head and shoulders pattern* had a higher middle peak than the triple top.

Continuation or Neutral Patterns

Symmetrical Triangles

Bullish

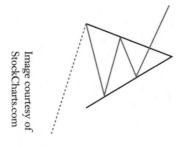

Bearish

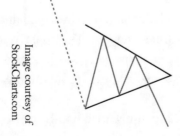

Symmetrical triangles look like the equilateral triangles we studied in geometry, yet since the financial world calls them symmetrical, that's the term we'll use. They are similar to wedges and pennants and can reverse a trend, but most often they continue the former trend direction. They are created by converging lines of support and resistance, one rising up and the other descending. As continuation or consolidation patterns, a balance between buyers and sellers, they usually last longer than a month and seldom last longer than three months.

The pattern is formed by a series of candlesticks, making lower highs and higher lows. This series should consist of two highs and two lows, each touching the trend line, for a minimum of four reversal points before the breakout, usually in the direction of its prior trend.

The *bullish pattern* has three peaks on the support line and two on resistance, breaking through resistance on the third touch. The *bearish pattern* has three peaks on the resistance line and two on the support line, breaking through support on the third touch. Within the pattern, other peaks may not touch the converging support and resistance lines; only peaks touching the lines are used in the count.

When the breakout finally does occur, it should be on increased volume as investors are at last certain about the direction of the market, releasing their pent-up supply and demand.

There are other chart patterns, but these are the most common. We'll now slip through our narrowing funnel to look at patterns as one candlestick relates to another or several others.

Candlestick Patterns–Bullish, Bearish, Reversal, and Neutral

Bullish

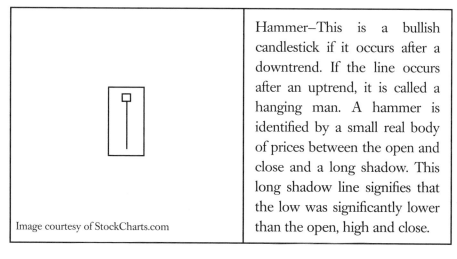

Image courtesy of StockCharts.com

Hammer–This is a bullish candlestick if it occurs after a downtrend. If the line occurs after an uptrend, it is called a hanging man. A hammer is identified by a small real body of prices between the open and close and a long shadow. This long shadow line signifies that the low was significantly lower than the open, high and close.

Image courtesy of StockCharts.com

Piercing Line—This is a bullish candlestick pattern and the opposite of a dark cloud cover. In this pattern, the first candlestick is a long red candle and the second candle is a long white. The second candle opens lower than the first, but it closes more than halfway above the first candle's real body.

Image courtesy of StockCharts.com

Bullish Engulfing—This is a strong bullish pattern if it occurs after a significant downtrend. It acts as a reversal pattern and occurs when a small red candle is engulfed by a large white candle.

Image courtesy of StockCharts.com

Morning Star—This is a bullish pattern that signals a potential bottom. The star indicates a possible reversal and the white candle confirms the signal. The star can be empty or hollow.

Image courtesy of StockCharts.com

Bullish Doji Star—A star indicates a reversal and a doji indicates indecision. Thus, this pattern usually indicates a reversal after a period of indecision and should be confirmed before entering a trade. The first candle can be filled or hollow.

Image courtesy of StockCharts.com	Three Black Crows–An odd name for three red candles that appear consecutively, closing near or below the previous candle's low. This is a bullish pattern.

Bearish

Image courtesy of StockCharts.com	Hanging Man–This is a bearish candlestick if it occurs after an uptrend.

Image courtesy of StockCharts.com	Dark Cloud Cover–This is a bearish pattern and is more significant if the second candle's body is below the center of the previous candle's body.

Image courtesy of StockCharts.com	Bearish Engulfing Candle– This is a strong bearish pattern if it occurs after a significant uptrend. It acts as a reversal pattern. It occurs when a small bullish white candle is engulfed by a large bearish red candle.

Image courtesy of StockCharts.com

Evening Star–This is a bearish pattern that signals a potential top. The star indicates a possible reversal and the red candle confirms this. The star can be red or white.

Image courtesy of StockCharts.com

Doji Star–A star indicates a reversal and a doji indicates indecision. Thus, this pattern usually points out a reversal following a period of indecision and should be confirmed before trading a doji star.

Image courtesy of StockCharts.com

Shooting Star–This pattern suggests a minor reversal when it appears after a rally. The star's body must appear near the candle's low and the candle should have along upper shadow.

Image courtesy of StockCharts.com

Three White Soldiers–This pattern consists of three relatively long white that close on or near their highs. This is a bearish pattern.

Reversal Patterns

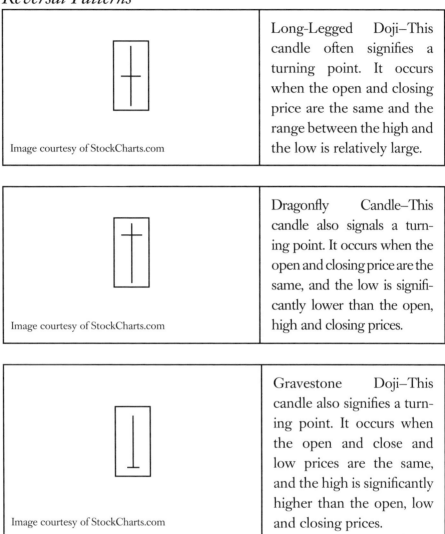

Image courtesy of StockCharts.com	Long-Legged Doji–This candle often signifies a turning point. It occurs when the open and closing price are the same and the range between the high and the low is relatively large.
Image courtesy of StockCharts.com	Dragonfly Candle–This candle also signals a turning point. It occurs when the open and closing price are the same, and the low is significantly lower than the open, high and closing prices.
Image courtesy of StockCharts.com	Gravestone Doji–This candle also signifies a turning point. It occurs when the open and close and low prices are the same, and the high is significantly higher than the open, low and closing prices.

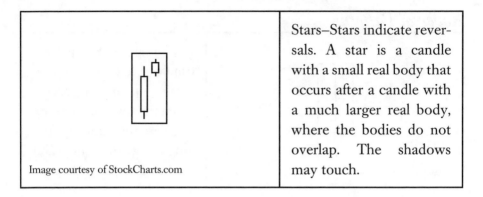

Image courtesy of StockCharts.com

Stars–Stars indicate reversals. A star is a candle with a small real body that occurs after a candle with a much larger real body, where the bodies do not overlap. The shadows may touch.

Neutral Patterns

Image courtesy of StockCharts.com

Spinning Tops–These are neutral candles. They occur when the distance between the high and low, and the distance between the open and close, are relatively small.

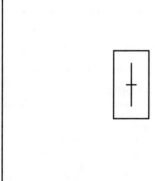

Image courtesy of StockCharts.com

Doji–This candle implies indecision. The security opened and closed at the same price. These candles appear in several different candle patterns.

Double Doji–Two adjacent dojis imply that a forceful move will follow a breakout from the current period of indecision.

Note: These are many of the most common candlestick shapes and patterns. If you are interested in learning more, StockCharts.com has a candlestick pattern dictionary.

Chapter Fourteen

Q&A WITH WENDY

Ever since Wendy began talking with other women about the exciting world of options, she's been asked the same questions again and again. We've listed some of these questions below and Wendy has answered them the same way she would in a seminar or within a small group. In some ways, these questions offer a glimpse into the personal side of trading and how trading options can fit into a woman's daily life.

Is there a daily or weekly routine or schedule that you follow?

After establishing my list of initial candidates—which I've redone periodically—I begin adding and deleting companies. For me, the weekends are the best time to spend a couple of hours reviewing the IBD and finding my new candidates and deleting others that have fallen from favor. Assuming I have money to invest, I review the IBD charts for stocks near new buy points and update my watch list. After studying the charts of those on my list, I choose which option I plan to buy the following week.

If I'm holding an option over from one week to the next, I look at its chart each evening, evaluating what I expect to happen and what my actions will be if it does or doesn't follow through. I base those decisions on the actions of the market as a whole, resistance and support levels on the security's chart, and the option's expiration date. I hold my sell point in mind, ready to act if it reaches that mark.

I try to check the market midday to check for the overall trend and for the performance of individual stocks. However, sometimes my schedule doesn't allow for a break and I'm forced to wait until late afternoon and am stuck with what the day brings. I evaluate again in the evening, standing ready to respond the next morning. As I come closer to an expiration date, nearing thirty days out, the more attention I pay to the individual investment, staying ready to sell at the highest profit.

Have your goals changed since you started option trading?

Yes, the way I think about the role of options has changed considerably. When I first became involved in option trading, my primary goal was to fund a retirement account with the idea that I would continue working for another five to ten years. Now I would like to trade options full time, meaning I would like to work a few hours a day managing my investments, allowing the options to not only fund my retirement account but to also provide a regular income.

What is your frame of mind–your mental approach–when you make an investment?

By nature I have a positive outlook on life. I approach my investments the same way. I expect to win and to make profits. Sometimes it doesn't happen, but I don't beat myself up over it. I certainly can't control the market's actions, but based on good research and chart reading skills I expect to be successful most of the time and I cut my losses short.

I project the intention of success and expect those results. I have a friend who approached her trading account with apprehension, even asking herself, "I wonder how much I lost today?" Her results often reflected her mindset. Then she'd berate herself with, "Why do I always make such bad choices?"

I advised my friend to change her expectations, practice virtual trading, and hold her funds for an option she felt positive about.

How are taxes on profits and losses handled?

You will keep track of your own trading transactions, of course. However, the brokerage firm also issues statements that tally your gains and losses, including year-end statements used to prepare your tax returns. Your results are declared on your tax return as investment income. Since income, offsetting expenses, and subsequent taxation is an individual situation based on so many varying factors, I advise going to a tax accountant or financial advisor who is familiar with your particular circumstances. In addition, option traders should remember to keep track of their expenses, such as the cost of a subscription to IBD or to StockCharts.com, as well as the brokerage fees that they pay.

Can you form a business around option trading?

I know several people who have incorporated or formed an LLC (Limited Liability Corporation) so they can handle their expenses and run their profits through a business entity. Quite often, these individuals have tied in other services into the company–newsletters, coaching, speaking services.

Looking at this question another way, you can view your option trading endeavor as a business right from the start, and as such, you'll use business tools to help you. You've taken a first step by buying this book. You'll visit relevant websites to begin learning; your subscription to IBD is another investment in education and training. Paper and virtual trading is your apprenticeship. Your lists and files are crucial to your businesslike organization, and your notations are part of record keeping you'll need to track success. The discipline of learning when to buy and sell is much like learning how to manage a business. And when you need a vacation, you can leave money in your trading account and relax without fretting about the market.

Is option trading completely an isolated, individual endeavor?

If you are asking if it's beneficial to have a trading buddy, someone to discuss strategies and chart reading with, then certainly, it's okay—in fact, it's a great idea and one of the main reasons we wrote this book. We want readers to use the tools, including our website and its discussion forums, as places to post successes. When you share and discuss experiences, you'll understand the process with greater ease and develop trading skills faster.

However, always remember that the trading decisions that you make are your own. No one else should be held responsible for your choices. In my area, groups of six or eight women traders have formed to share potential candidates' charts, but each woman trades alone.

Option trading doesn't put you in competition with others. If you take a slice or two of the pie, that doesn't mean there are fewer pieces available for everyone else. In addition, this is not like having a career in which you have to protect yourself from others climbing the corporate ladder—and your job looks like one of the rungs. It's also not like a business where demand is limited and only a certain number of customers exist, and you must fight for your market share within the industry. With option trading, we know there's plenty to go around and there's no reason to hoard or protect information as if it's top secret. The more open interest there is in a particular option, the better; therefore, it's fine to share thoughts on an option candidate or its chart. But, don't act on advice about an option without doing your homework and checking it out yourself.

What qualities do you think good traders share?

First, I think good traders need to *like* trading options. Just like anything else worthwhile, the process is easier and smooth if you enjoy it. I manage to muster a good attitude toward cleaning my house when I need to, but I'd be miserable if I'd gone into the cleaning business. But, the truth is, I'd rather earn money trading options so I can hire someone else to clean my house.

Good option traders need to reach a place of emotional stability with their trading. It's a place of balance. They need to be able to assess a candidate without emotions involved–this is strictly an intellectual or cognitive process. Then their decisions to buy are based on sound analysis, not fear of missing out on a profit or greed of chasing something that's already happened. That emotional balance extends to sell decisions, and solid traders cut losses short and don't hold profits as they look for more, even when the chart says it is time to sell.

When good traders experience a loss, they maintain that stable-trader attitude, knowing a loss is just a small bump along the path to financial empowerment. There will be a greater number of successful trades. In the end, the pluses outweigh the minuses, the gains outweigh the losses.

Once a good trader establishes a trading plan, she works the plan and sticks to the rules. She doesn't second-guess herself.

Are you involved in the market all the time?

I try to be aware of what is happening in the market each day, but I am not invested or holding options every day. Sometimes the market atmosphere is too volatile and it's too difficult to clearly read the signs. During those periods, I will sit on the sideline, holding money in my account. I can't lose money while I'm waiting for a good chance to jump back in.

Since I still read *Investors Business Daily* and other financial reports, trying to stay abreast of what is driving the market, I know from experience that things will settle down and new buying opportunities are just over the horizon. It seems that all traders must learn this lesson. We all experience a nagging feeling that if we're not in the game by having our investment dollars working, then we're losing a money-making opportunity. At times this may turn out to be the case, but more often, if we have strong reservations and are uncomfortable, we're probably sparing ourselves unnecessary losses.

Do some women trade only ETFs?

Yes, many women like the risk-ratio of Exchange Traded Funds. Since ETFs do not function on one security's performance, they do not suffer the same fluctuations. They are a composite, a basket of numerous entities, intentionally combined to perform as a whole.

Do you have a favorite stock or a list of stocks you particularly like?

It's hard not to have a few stocks that you favor, especially if you have profited from them. That said, never hold a stock past its sell signal just because it's a favorite. At times, I've fought these maternal instincts over my option choices. If I sold, I felt like I was abandoning it, as if I'd lost confidence in its ability to perform. No kidding, I've actually had those feelings. But I eventually forced myself to practice tough love and push it out of my investment nest, knowing I could invite it in again at some future point if it started to look like a good investment again.

How do you handle losses on an emotional level?

I've found that the best way to handle loss situations is to make every effort to keep them as small as possible. A minor loss is easier to carry home, more palatable, and far more digestible. Yet, loss is part of the option game. We must accept loss, but not expect it. Losses are a side effect of being involved in a stock market where we don't have real control over any part of it.

I don't know any investor who wins all the time. Here's an example. Let's say we made five investments of $500 each, and then two of them doubled, making 100% gains. With two others, we cut our losses short at 25%, but the fifth investment lost half its value. Even though out of the five options only two gained (less than half), we netted $250 or 10% of our initial $2500 investment. This emphasizes the importance of cutting losses quickly.

How much of your investment fund do you have invested at any one time? And how much on any one stock?

As my account grows, I withdraw funds to invest in my retirement account and I have taken money for unexpected expenses, but I try to have my investing funds multiplying. I keep most of my fund working when the market is up-trending, though as I've said before, I will pull back or not be invested at all if the environment is too uncertain. I never invest more than half of my account in one option. It is too easy for an equity to sour and have its option decline. If all my funds were all tied up in that one equity and I failed to get out quickly, my investment fund would be depleted.

Do you watch the stock channels on TV? And if so, how do you filter the information?

I sometimes tune in as I'm getting ready for work in the morning and listen to opinions offered by guests or analysts. These discussions are often orchestrated as a debate with varying takes on the subject being discussed. My ears perk up at the scheduled reports–labor numbers, unemployment reports, *Fed. Tuesday* once a month, GDP numbers, and so forth, because these figures often dictate how the day will go. I also watch the crawls across the screen of the Dow, NASDAQ, and S&P futures.

If an option contract drops to the point that it has no value at its expiration date, do you have to close it, so that you don't have to exercise the option and buy the stock?

Remember that an option by definition allows you to buy the underlying stock, but does not obligate you to do so. If an option has no value or less value than the cost of the fees needed to close it, let it expire worthless. There is no reason to pay the broker a fee to close an option that is worthless. The next business day after expiration, the option will be removed from your account.

Are there option traders who day trade?

Yes, some traders become so involved they are in and out of trades over short periods of time. Some hold their options for a few days, less than a day, and even for only an hour or so.

OptionsXpress allows you to move in and out of the trade within the same day, a total of three times (three trades) a week, before they consider you a day trader. Day trader's accounts have different guidelines, such as having to maintain a minimum balance of $20,000–$25,000.

When you sell an option contract, are those funds available immediately to reinvest?

No, or at least not at *optionsXpress*. It takes time to process the transaction and for the funds to be deposited into your account. At *optionsXpress,* the funds are available the next business day. I have learned, though, that *optionsXpress* will make exceptions on occasion. If you call or click on *live help* and ask that the funds be made available for immediate use, they will release the funds as long as you agree to hold and not sell the new transactions for three days. There are definitely times that this would pay, but don't make these arrangements on an option that you are not confident will advance or doesn't have the benefit of time.

What would you say is the most valuable lesson you have learned?

I had to learn not to let greed win out–that is, holding on to an option, hoping for a little more profit. For me, the discipline of trading involved establishing a line in the sand that was a sell point when I held a profit. If a stock retreated to cross that line, no matter what, once it hit that mark, I sold. I counted myself lucky for having earned a profit, whatever the amount over my expenses, and I never looked back in the subsequent days to see what could have been. If I judged my decision to sell by what I missed, I knew that would then influence my decisions in the future. There is no guarantee the next occasion would produce the same results. I follow my self-imposed rule and stick to it!

What would you say has been your biggest mistake?

My biggest mistake–and I've made it several times–relates to the last question. There have been a few occasions when I've made a sizable profit and held on too long. One of those times I earned $1,500 on an $1,800 investment, nearly 100%. But, when the stock dropped a little I held it, thinking it surely would go back up the next day. Then it dropped more, and still more. I, forever hopeful that it would rise again to its old level, held so long that I not only lost all my profit, I held until I started losing my invested money. I couldn't make myself let go. It was then that I developed my line in the sand rule.

Everyone has to come up with a formula that works for them based on their tolerance of risk and loss. For me, if I have a profit, the line is a drop below the 20 on the Williams %R. If the stock drops below that line and I have less than three months left (which really means two months if I plan to sell 30 days out from expiration), I sell. I know I can always buy it again if it reverses. I will then also benefit from buying at a lower point. However, if or when it drops below my sell line, it may well be dropping to form a new base. If it does that, it will probably last at least seven weeks (nearly two months), so, therefore, to assume it will rise to its old level in a week or less is foolishness and more risk than I am willing to take–ever again.

Can a person make a living trading options?

Many people start trading options part-time, using it to accomplish some specific goal or objective, and then move into full-time trading to earn a living. They've discovered that they can work fewer hours and earn more by letting their investment funds do most of the work. This is the place I've reached, having decided that option trading can provide a real monthly income.

GLOSSARY

A

accumulation: The act of buying shares of a security by institutions or professional investors over a period of time to avoid forcing the market higher with a single purchase. After a decline, a security's price may start to form a base and trade sideways for an extended period of time. While this base forms, traders and investors may seek to establish long or call positions. The stock is said to have come under accumulation.

annual earnings: This term refers to a company's earnings per share during a particular year. Most companies report earnings quarterly, and then report the year's earnings at the end of their fiscal year.

ask price: This is the price at which a market buy order will usually be filled. It is higher that the bid price (sell order) and is set by market makers based on supply and demand.

at-the-close: The price at which a security is traded at the end of the trading day.

at-the-money: An option is said to be at-the-money if the strike price is the same as the stock's or Index's current market price. At-the-money options have no intrinsic value, unlike in-the-money.

at-the-open: The price at which a security is trading at the beginning of the trading day.

B

bears: A bear or bearish investor believes prices will decline. When bears win over the bulls, prices move lower. We're in a bearish market when a large percentage of all securities within the major indices decline for an extended period of time.

bid price: The minimum price at which a market sell order will usually be filled. It is lower than the ask price and is set by the market makers based on supply and demand.

blue chip: A stock is considered *blue chip* when it's a well-known company with long-term reputation for quality and good fundamentals. Many stocks once thought of as blue chips can become sluggish as they grow too big and become stuck in a prescribed performance rut.

breakout: A move in which a stock rises past a buy point, usually on a surge of volume. It is the best place for stock buyers and option buyers to purchase a leading stock or index or options on that underlying instrument. Breakouts often occur near a new price high. During a breakout, a stock's price shoots past a level where it has run into resistance. It often occurs after a stock has undergone a consolidation and formed a base, then breaks out past the pattern's buy point.

bulls: A bull or a bullish investor believes prices will rise. When the bulls win over the bears, prices move higher. A bullish market is one in which a high percentage of all securities within the major indices move higher for an extended period of time.

buy point: A price level considered to have low risk, based on past performance of leading stocks. Most buy points are based on resistance levels in a base, such as a handle. This is a place of least upward resistance, breaking out to a new high.

buying range: A price area determined from a stock's or index's test of the 50-day SMA (ten-week) line. It extends from that test point to 5% past the high the stock made just prior to the pullback.

C

call: A stock option that gives the right but not the obligation to buy a certain stock at a certain price by a certain date.

candlesticks: A symbol that represents price information over time. Within a chart, each candlestick reflects price activity for a certain period, such as a day or a week. The body of the candlestick indicates the opening and closing prices and is filled if the price closed lower than the open. It is hollow or unfilled if it closed higher than the opening price. The thin lines or shadows above and below the candle indicate price fluctuations throughout the period.

channel: A defined area in which a security's price fluctuates–the upper line is referred to as resistance (demand) and the lower is support (supply). We plot lines by drawing a straight line that connects three of the stocks highest candles (prices) and another line connecting three low candles (prices). These lines usually cover a period of several months.

contrary indicator: These are signals that flash what most people–or too many people–are doing, which may be a clue that the opposite event is apt to happen.

D

defensive stocks or sectors: These are less volatile stocks and sectors that are not as vulnerable to economic swings as others stocks or groups. They include utilities, supermarkets, tobacco, toilet tissue, and soap products, all of which represent consumer staples and repeat, predictable business. Food, household goods, energy, are included as well, but these sectors have a limited upside because of their lower volatility. Defensive stocks or sectors are more popular when the broad market is in a decline.

delta: The amount by which the option will move if the underlying security moves one point.

distribution day: A decline in a major stock index of more than 0.2% as volume increases over the prior day. Multiple distribution days in a short-span of time (2–4 weeks) may signal the start of a market downturn.

distribution: Distribution occurs when a stock falls in price on volume greater than the day before. Option traders should purchase puts and target stocks under bouts of distribution and when the market has numerous distribution days, perhaps leading to a market correction.

E

earnings growth: A company's rate of profit growth either for the quarter compared with the same period a year earlier or for the full year compared with the year before.

exchange traded funds: Exchange traded funds are a group or basket of stocks that are bought and sold together under their own symbol. ETFs are generally thought of as less risky than individual stocks.

exercising an option: This means to actually buy or sell the underlying security that the option covers. We as option traders never exercise the option, but simply trade the rights to it.

exhaustion gap: This occurs when a stock's price gaps up from the prior day's high close after a long, powerful price advance lasting several months or more. This often indicates the last stage of a run-up.

expiration date: The date at which an option expires; it is the third Friday of the expiration month named in the option.

extended: Investors Business Daily uses this term in combination with a percentage to describe how far a stock has traveled beyond its buy point. IBD advises that stocks extended 5% beyond their buy point should not be considered for stock purchase. This is stock chasing and should be avoided.

F

flat base: We commonly see this after a stock has broken out of a cup and handle or double bottom base. The stock's price goes sideways on a tight range for at least five weeks and corrects 8%–12% upward in price.

52-week high: This is highest price at which a stock has traded during the previous fifty-two weeks. The price is adjusted for any stock splits that may have occurred.

float: The number of shares outstanding on a company's stock available for trading by the general public. Generally, stocks with small floats have an easier time making big price moves. However, a small float can discourage the pack from purchasing because they may want to take or leave a position without disturbing the price. Their volume would swing the price drastically either up or down. Float is also used in connection to options and the time that a broker needs to fill an option order at a limit price.

fundamental analysis: This refers to what we might call the basics and evaluates a company's earnings, return on equity (ROE), profit margins, share of the market, and other fundamental numbers. Fundamental analysis goes hand-in-hand with technical analysis.

G

gap: A gap occurs when a stock opens and trades well above or below the prior day's trading range.

gamma: This is the delta of the delta–the amount of change in the delta of the option when the stock changes in price by a point.

H

historical volatility: This is a strict statistical measure of how fast prices have changed in the past.

I

Investors Business Daily *(IBD):* This is the newspaper commonly used to screen stocks.

implied volatility: This is an estimate of how volatile the underlying will be during the life of the option.

index or sector options: These are options on an index, such as the S&P 100, or on a sector, such as the Semiconductor Index.

indicator: Technical tools used to analyze price and volume data that are used to try to anticipate the direction a security will head next, based on where it has been and its current activity. There are two kinds of indicators–lagging (following) and momentum (leading).

insider trading: This term refers to trading based on advance knowledge of a corporate event. It's not a legal way to trade.

institutional investors: The *tutes* include mutual funds, banks, insurance companies, pension funds, and other large investors. Their activity comprises most of the trading volume, and in turn their actions often determine price movement of stocks or indexes.

in-the-money: An option is said to be in-the-money when the strike price is below the stock's or index's current market price. In-the-money options are priced higher than at- or out-of-the-money options because of their intrinsic or built-in value.

intrinsic value: One of two components of option pricing, this is the amount by which a call is in-the-money. The strike price minus market price equals the intrinsic value. The *ask premium* minus the *intrinsic value* equals the *time value.*

initial public offering (IPO): Often referred to as *going public,* this is the first offering of a corporation's stock for public purchase.

L

laggard: See *leader.*

late-stage base: A fourth-stage or later price consolidation, forming a base that occurs late in a stock's overall advance. This is a warning sign that a stock may be exhausting itself and will soon be reversing into a long-term decline.

leader: A company that is either outperforming the general stock market (leader) or underperforming the market (laggard). These terms are also used in reference to industry groups that are outperforming or under-performing the market.

limit order: An order to be executed at a specified price or better. An order placed with limitations on price or on a time to be filled. As an example, a limit order could specify that an option order is not to be filled at the market price, but only when the price reaches a specified price by a specified time.

liquidity: The ability of a stock or security to withstand heavy buying and selling without undergoing major fluctuations in price. Indications of liquidity include high volume and high open interest on the option chains, meaning lots of buyers and sellers.

long: In our option world, to *long* the market means to buy calls or sell puts.

Long-term Equity AnticiPation Securities (LEAPS): LEAPS are options that feature an extended period of time to expiration, usually longer than nine months.

M

margin account: A brokerage account in which the brokerage firm will lend the client a percentage of the equity to purchase additional security positions.

market maker: An independent trader or trading firm that stands ready to buy or sell contracts in a designated market. Market markers determine and quote both a buy and sell price in an underlying instrument, hoping to make a profit on the bid/ask spread.

market order: An order that is placed to buy or sell an option on a security at the current market price. It usually fills immediately at the current ask (buy) price or sell (bid) price.

moving average line: The average of a stock's price or volume over a period of time. A daily stock chart will often include seven, twenty, and fifty-day moving averages; the weekly chart includes fifty-day and two-hundred-day moving averages. The IBD often uses the ten-week line. These lines can serve as support levels for stocks in an uptrend, and as a level of resistance for stocks in downtrends.

N

NASDAQ Composite Index: An index of over five thousand stocks, it's dominated by technology stocks, including the computer industry. COMP is the ticker symbol used for the NASDAQ Composite Index.

NASDAQ 100 Index: A market-capitalization-weighted index of the biggest non-financial companies on the NASDAQ exchange. The QQQQ is the ticker symbol for the NASDAQ-100 Index tracking stock.

O

open interest: This reflects the number of contracts currently held on an option. As open interest increases, more money is flowing into that option.

option: An option is the right, but not the obligation, to buy or sell a security at a given price before a specified expiration date.

oscillators: Momentum or leading indicators that track relative price or volume performance for a security over a certain period of time. They move up and down into overbought and oversold territories that reflect highs and lows.

out-of-the-money: The term used when a call option's strike price is in excess of the current market price of the underlying security. In the case of a put option, it would be the amount below the current market price.

P

paper trading: Tracking pretend option trades to test one's investing techniques without risking real money.

percentage price oscillator (PPO): An indicator based on the difference between two moving averages and expressed as a percentage (See *oscillator.*)

pullback: A price retreat that takes a stock back near a moving average, sometimes after and during an uptrend or a breakout.

put-call ratio: All the puts traded on a particular day divided by the total of all the calls traded on that same day.

put: A stock option that gives the right, but not the obligation, to sell a certain stock or index at a certain price by a certain time.

R

range: The area between a high price and the low price of a stock or index for a given period of time.

relative strength: The relationship of a stock's price to the Dow Jones Industrial Average, NASDAQ, or other grouping. The indicator is designed to show how a stock is performing relative to the other stocks as compared to the market or industry average.

resistance: This is a price level which a stock shows a tendency to stay below, so resistance can be likened to a ceiling. A stock may climb to this level and then stall. Moving above resistance on heavy volume is a bullish sign or action.

Russell 2000 Index: A capitalization-weighted market index comprised of the smallest two thousand firms in the Russell 3000. This index is widely regarded as the premium measure of small-cap stocks.

S

S&P 500 Index ($SPX): Standard and Poor's Index for five hundred of the largest stocks from major companies in a variety of industries.

sector index: An index whose stocks belong to a certain sector, such as gold, oil, steel, or healthcare.

shake out: A sharp decline in a stock that had been rising. Usually a key buy point is breached on the way down, sparking stop-loss selling or shaking out those fearful of losing their profit, thus causing them to sell.

short: A position whose holder will benefit by a decrease in the security's value.

short the market: This refers to selling calls to close a position or buying puts to open a position.

simple moving average (SMA): A moving average that gives equal weight to each day's price movement, as opposed to more heavily weighted open or close prices.

slippage: If you buy at the ask and sell at the bid prices, the difference (loss), along with the commission paid, is referred to as slippage.

spread. This usually refers to the difference between bid and ask premiums.

stochastics oscillator: A momentum indicator that measures the price of a security relative to its own high/low range over a certain period of time. Its movement runs into overbought and oversold ranges, giving buy and sell signals.

stop-loss selling: A sell order will cause a stock to be sold if it falls below a certain price, usually placed to limit losses.

strike price. The price at which an option may be exercised.

support: This is a price level that a stock has shown a tendency to stay above, so it can be considered a floor. Support often occurs at key moving averages. Support at the 50 SMA is a place where institutions often buy shares after a pullback, giving their support to a stock. This support is enough to stop the downward movement, and bring about a move back up.

T

technical analysis: An evaluation of a stock's price and volume movements, usually on a stock chart, to analyze buying and selling in the market.

theta: The amount of change in the option price when one day passes. Theta can also be referred to as time decay on the value of an option. The option loses value as time moves closer to its expiration date.

thin stock: IBD's term for a stock with an average daily volume of about one hundred thousand shares or less. The institutional investors—the pack—tend to ignore stocks trading with so few shares.

ticker symbol: This is the abbreviation used to identify a company listed on the stock exchange. You've no doubt noted that the charts in this book use the ticker symbols.

time value: This refers to the portion of the option's premium that exceeds the intrinsic value.

trade candidate filter: A stock screening method that uses information supplied by the IBD newspaper.

trading market: In a trading market, prices move in a choppy up-and-down fluctuating pattern, generally sideways with no apparent major trend.

trading system: A trading method that uses well-defined rules for entry and exit points.

trailing stop: A stop that moves with the position when it is making money, but remains static if it is losing money. It triggers the sale of a stock at a level determined by the investor. This allows the order to trail behind a rising stock for the purpose of locking in option profits.

triple witching: The days in which futures, options on stocks, and options on stock indexes expire on the same day. It occurs on the third Friday in March, June, September, and December. This usually results in higher volatility and higher volume.

U

underlying instrument: The stock, index, ETF, or futures contract on which options are traded.

V

vega: The amount of change in the option price when volatility moves up or down by one percentage point.

virtual trading: Trading online to practice, but without using money. All the aspects of trading are experienced except the emotions brought on by real profits or losses.

volatility: This term refers to the upward and downward movement of the market or a particular security.

volume: The number of shares bought or sold. Volume measures conviction behind a move; big jumps in volume indicate that the professionals, the institutions, are buying.

W

wedging: A technical term for an upward price pattern in the handle of a cup-shaped base. The pattern lasts at least a week. This is a negative pattern, as proper handles show a minor downtrend before a breakout. Handles that wedge upward are prone to failure.

whipsaws: This refers to choppy up-and-down price movement reflected in indicators, often seen during a trading market, but can also be seen under trending conditions. Whipsaws are more evident in shorter time periods (7-day SMA), whereas indicators reflecting a longer time period (50-day SMA) tend to be smoother.

Williams %R: This is a momentum indicator that swings between overbought and oversold conditions, giving buy and sell signals as it moves out of an area.

APPENDIX:
USEFUL WEBSITES

We want you to have many resources at your disposal. We've mentioned some of these websites in various places in the book; others provide additional information about various companies. Keep this list handy for quick reference.

WomenOptionTraders.com

Investors.com

Finance.Yahoo.com

BigCharts.com

StockCharts.com

optionsXpress.com

Earnings.com

Morningstar.com

Hoovers.com

Signalwatch.com

INDEX

ABOUT THE AUTHORS

Wendy Kirkland and her husband, Jack, own Legacies, a gift shop in the heart of historic Biltmore Village in Asheville, North Carolina. Long before she developed an interest in option trading, Wendy was an award-winning artist, carver, and sculptor. Today, she's passionate about writing and supporting other women's quest to enter the world of option trading through the website, WomenOptionTraders.com, which offers online workshops. Wendy also enjoys spending time with her three children and six grandchildren.

A writer for over thirty years, **Virginia McCullough** specializes in coauthoring and ghostwriting books with experts in various fields. Recent books include *The Oxygen Revolution* (with Paul Harch, MD) and *52 Bright Ideas to Bring More Humor, Hugs, and Hope into Your Life* (with Greg Risberg, MSW). The mother of two grown children, Virginia currently lives in Green Bay, Wisconsin.

Ameritrade Screens

① 7, 20, 50 Day Moving AGS
       p. 54 (Crossovers)

② Relative strength Index
       p. 56

p. 140 Trailing stops — close
     position at $ amount
       or % loss

p. 141 streaming charts

The Plan — p. 167